LOYAL: LISTEN OR YOU ALWAYS LOSE

LOYAL

[**Listen** Or You Always Lose]

A LEADER'S GUIDE TO
WINNING CUSTOMER AND
EMPLOYEE LOYALTY

AARON PAINTER

COPYRIGHT © 2017 AARON PAINTER
All rights reserved.

LOYAL: LISTEN OR YOU ALWAYS LOSE
A Leader's Guide to Winning Customer and Employee Loyalty

ISBN   978-1-61961-751-3 *Hardcover*
        978-1-61961-752-0 *Paperback*
        978-1-61961-753-7 *Ebook*

To my team members, colleagues and friends, who invite me to listen.

CONTENTS

INTRODUCTION 9

1. SPECIALIZATION BREEDS CHOICE 27
2. CURIOSITY LEADS TO UNDERSTANDING 51
3. RESPECT BUILDS TRUST 79
4. LOYALTY BRINGS CONSISTENCY 111
5. LISTENING FUELS INNOVATION 145
6. CULTURE DRIVES TRANSFORMATION 171
7. PEOPLE SUSTAIN GROWTH 203
8. TECHNOLOGY EMPOWERS PEOPLE 241

CONCLUSION: THE LOYAL ORGANIZATION ... 271

ACKNOWLEDGMENTS 277

ABOUT THE AUTHOR 281

REFERENCES 285

INTRODUCTION

*Customers will never love a company
until the employees love it first.*

—SIMON SINEK, AUTHOR, SPEAKER, AND
LEADERSHIP CONSULTANT

How often do you buy something and walk away feeling good about the person or company you purchased from? How often do you leave work feeling that your contributions are appreciated? Perhaps there are times when you'd like to offer feedback, as a customer or as an employee, that you think could improve the experience of others. Yet, you may not be sure how to share that feedback, and you may doubt that, if you do, anyone from the company will listen. Most of us rarely consider issues like these until a new opportunity arises, in the form of a new business, or maybe even a new employer, that seems to offer a better alternative. By then, it's often too late.

Now, more than ever, businesses that want to cultivate sustained business growth need your loyalty. Loyalty is more than simple satisfaction; it is a strong feeling of support or allegiance to something or someone. Earning and maintaining loyalty begins with listening, a skill that any business or individual can prioritize from the beginning of a relationship. Employees who feel that their perspectives are heard and understood can grow to become committed and loyal. Those employees will represent the companies and brands that employ them by being equally good listeners, giving those companies the power to recruit committed, loyal customers.

In years gone by, loyalty was engendered by regular personal contact. A customer could walk into a local grocery store, hardware store, or clothing retailer, and be welcomed by an owner or clerk who knew them, listened to them, and was invested in understanding and providing for their needs.

As communities became more dispersed, businesses grew larger and potential markets increased in size. Many companies found that they could become more profitable by scaling their operations, developing new products, and acquiring additional customers. Often, a competitive advantage could be gained by cutting costs and lowering prices.

That's changing, and fast. Around the world, even in developing markets, which were once popularly thought of as an endless source of cheap labor and new business, expanding a business's customer base and acquiring skilled and loyal employees is becoming more and more difficult. Instead, businesses recognize a greater need for loyalty in order to develop more powerful relationships with existing customers and employees. Additionally, technology is changing the way we listen, opening up new vistas and possibilities.

My personal and professional background has given me a front row seat to the transformation taking place in the global economy. I've worked at Microsoft for nearly fourteen years, and today, I'm one of the most global business leaders in one of the world's most global companies. I've lived and worked in both North and South America, along with Europe and Asia, and traveled to more than a hundred countries, all before my thirtieth birthday. I feel incredibly fortunate to have learned so much about the world, and to have witnessed firsthand the ways smart companies use technology to empower people and catalyze change.

The idea for this book came to me approximately five years ago, when I moved to China. It was a move that opened my eyes even wider to the transformation underway. I quickly realized that the country, its people, and its methods of doing business would have a huge influence in shaping the world for the rest of my lifetime.

This book is about more than either China or Microsoft, however. It is about what I've learned and experienced from meeting with and listening to business leaders from a broad range of industries and companies, all around the world. Time and again, I discover that their greatest challenges lie in the realm of loyalty, although perhaps not in the way you might expect.

I came to realize that traditional practices of engagement, with customers and employees alike, are key to building a successful business, and that those practices start with listening. Simultaneously, however, advances in technology are taking place incredibly fast, extending an invitation to us all to use these new tools to listen and engage even more effectively.

LOYALTY: A KEY MINDSET IN THE TWENTY-FIRST CENTURY ORGANIZATION

Mention loyalty to some business executives, and they will

assume that you're referring to loyalty programs, offering customers discounts and special offers when they spend a certain amount of money with the company.

While these programs can be useful, the concept of loyalty described in this book goes far deeper than the kind of rewards promoted by a loyalty program. It extends to every interaction between management and employees, and employees and customers.

I meet representatives from dozens of companies who want to cultivate loyalty, and whose first impulse is to create a loyalty program or a membership program. As we discuss what loyalty really means to them, it soon becomes clear that it is a very powerful word, and that a loyalty program only captures a fraction of the intent behind developing loyalty.

Most loyalty programs don't change company culture. As such, they don't have a significant impact upon employee retention, or the way employees engage with customers. They're valuable in their own right, but they simply cannot resolve all the challenges these companies are facing. That takes a commitment to relate to employees and customers with respect and curiosity. A commitment to listen.

In Asia, the bedrock of the local economy is the family-run business. Generally speaking, family-run businesses perceive their operations on a very long timescale. Their objectives are to pass on a healthy, functioning business to the next generation. They're not usually public, so they don't operate under the pressure of generating dividends every quarter.

Family businesses are set up to deliver long-term, sustained growth rather than short-term profits to shareholders. The only way to do that is through winning trust and cultivating loyalty. They remind us that being a good businessperson is remarkably similar to being a good sibling or a good parent. The good parent and the good businessperson both prioritize long-term relationships.

Building long-term relationships is vital in order to institute growth. Growth requires change, and it's extremely difficult to manage change successfully without trust. Why? Because change inevitably involves some degree of risk.

Whether you're creating new products, marketing those products differently, or expanding into entirely new markets, you will undoubtedly confront uncertainty. To navigate uncertainty successfully, you must be able to trust the people around you. Risk-taking only becomes practical in an environment of trust.

Loyalty enables lasting change. It also enables employee retention. The same factors that make a company successful, make employees of that company appealing to other firms.

Committed, loyal staff members will stay, knowing that they are valued uniquely in their existing role and that the relationships they have built with their team will take considerable time and effort to replace. Others will leave, costing the company both directly and indirectly as new staff members adapt to the novel environment.

Short-term growth is relatively simple to catalyze. A team of smart people brought in to locate cost savings, or ways to boost sales, will probably succeed. If that team leaves, however, other parts of the organization may find it very difficult to replicate their success. That's why sustainable business growth relies on loyalty.

In America, mom and pop businesses sometimes seem to be floundering, crushed by huge supermarkets and giant corporations that can gain enormous cost savings by scaling their operations. Globally, however, family-owned businesses are on the rise. A recent study in *The Economist* [1] revealed that 15 percent of all businesses were family-owned in 2010, and predicted that number would grow to 40 percent by 2025.

INTRODUCTION · 15

These numbers partially reflect business culture in Asia, where family businesses are very common and growing. The *values* that drive the growth of family businesses, however, can be applied to any team or organization, leading to similarly successful outcomes. Even larger organizations can utilize the lessons of family businesses to behave more like them in the realms of trust and loyalty. It takes work, and it takes genuine commitment, but it is possible.

Fortunately, technology that enables the cultivation of loyalty is developing at a staggering pace. As fast as organizations are realizing the essential importance of listening to their employees and customers, so too are digital solutions being created that allow them to do so.

This intersection of traditional wisdom and technological advancement is opening up exciting new horizons for businesses that want to scale their operations and grow their reach while continuing to treat every customer, and every employee, with respect.

DIGITAL TRANSFORMATION IN THE FOURTH INDUSTRIAL REVOLUTION

The trends outlined in this book are not unique to my experiences, and in fact, some thought leaders have already sought to name this new era of business. Klaus Schwab, founder and executive chairman of the World Economic Forum, published a book prior to their annual conference in Davos, Switzerland, at the start of 2016. His thesis was that we are now entering a Fourth Industrial Revolution.

The First Industrial Revolution can be traced back to 1784 and the advent of water and steam power. The second commenced in the 1870s with the division of labor and mass production. The third stems from 1969 with automated production, electronics, and IT. The Fourth Industrial Revolution is happening right now, and it's a digital revolution.

As the speed of technology increases, and new innovations blur the boundaries between disciplines, between the physical and the digital, and maybe even between the digital and the biological, the Fourth Industrial Revolution has astounding potential to alter the way we relate to our businesses and to one another.

Many of the Chinese companies I work with are already discovering this. The firms they see as competitors are the ones that have already embraced digital technologies, and they're finding that those technologies give them a competitive edge.

In the Fourth Industrial Revolution, data is becoming the

new electricity; the driving force that powers our activities. The quantity of data available to us today is mind-blowing. A few years ago, a global market intelligence firm, IDC, made headlines by predicting that the total quantity of digital data created worldwide would mushroom from 4.4 zettabytes in 2013 to 44 zettabytes by 2020.[2] At the time of publication, IDC projects that this number will rise to 180 zettabytes by 2025. To give you an idea of how much data this represents, 44 zettabytes is equivalent to 250 billion DVDs, or 36 million *years* of HD video.

The astonishing growth stems from the sheer number of devices connecting to the Internet. At present, there are approximately eleven billion, but this number could reach thirty billion by 2020 and eighty billion by 2025. This explosion of data is driving new forms of connection, such as digital phone calls and cloud computing. It's also inviting us to harness that data for an extraordinary range of purposes.

Another facet of the Fourth Industrial Revolution is that its adoption is relatively flat; it's spreading very quickly across the globe. This distinguishes it from the first three industrial revolutions, which were far more unevenly distributed.

Many people, when they consider the concept of a digital

revolution, think in terms of having a website or using technology to run their organization. True digital transformation requires businesses to build intelligent systems or even new business models, often leading to change in profound ways. It requires the sophistication and deepening of processes that are already part of the business, such as ordering, accounting, mobile apps, or ERP (Enterprise Resource Planning). All these systems can be connected to central nodes, for example a cloud, enabling analysis of the data to a previously unthinkable degree.

For most businesses, a strategy of digital transformation consists of four components: improved engagement with customers; deeper understanding and empowerment of employees; product improvement, and operations optimization.

Many make the mistake of focusing their technological strategies primarily on product improvement and operations optimization. The downside of that strategy is that, unless companies also engage more effectively with customers and employees, product improvement and operations optimization alone won't attract loyal customers and employees.

The combination of technology, people, and process is an extremely potent one. Organizations that are changing the landscapes of their industries are utilizing all three of these tools to secure a competitive edge.

At Microsoft, our mission from inception has been to assist people in realizing their potential. There was a time when that meant putting a PC on every desk or in every home. Since then, personal computing technology has developed from the dreams of Bill Gates, Paul Allen, and others to a reality, connecting billions of people around the world.

Over the last few years, we've been transforming our own business through data. We use listening technologies to monitor how people use our products and shape the way we improve them. We cultivate a culture that encourages managers to listen to employees. Now we're helping other organizations that want to understand and harness the power of digital transformation.

All of this is not to say that you shouldn't have a website. For most businesses, a website is an essential tool. Digital transformation is much bigger, however, and much more exciting than simply having an online presence. It is driven both by a shift in technology and a shift in mindset. Almost every organization is becoming an IT-powered organization.

THE BUSINESS CASE FOR LOYALTY

In a recent study of business leaders worldwide,[3] conducted by American research and advisory firm Gartner, over half of the respondents indicated that they expected their businesses to be digital by 2017. The same study said that over 75 percent of CEOs expected digital transformation to result in higher profit,[4] while 65 percent of them felt they had not yet made significant progress on that journey.

The term "digital" refers not only to technology, but also to the ways businesses can use modern advances in computing to change or create entirely new business models.

Technology products and the companies who make or sell them are only one part of the equation, but they demonstrate how business models are changing. Hardware products such as laptops, tablets, and mobile phones are relatively cheap to build or acquire. Even when they keep margins as high as possible, manufacturers and retailers make a comparatively small profit on selling hardware to their customers. In addition, the real value of digital products lies in making them highly accessible, both because of what they allow customers to achieve, and because most digital business models are based on usage.

Many companies are prepared to break even on mobile handsets, or even give them away as part of a fixed-term contract, because the success of their businesses is based not on the number of units they sell, but on the usage of services such as phone minutes, texts, Internet data, and apps.

In a world where more and more business models are based on usage, business leaders realize that simply finding more and more customers won't keep them competitive. They need to develop *relationships* with their customers that extend far beyond the initial purchase.

To borrow a phrase from business terminology, sustainable organizations in the twenty-first century focus less on individual sales and more on the *lifetime value* of customers. That lifetime value depends almost entirely on how the company is perceived, both internally and externally, and on the degree to which both employees and customers are motivated to sustain a relationship with the company.

In this market, companies that invest a lot of time, energy and money in convincing customers to buy a product, only to immediately switch their attention to another customer and neglect the ongoing relationship, will fail both to connect meaningfully with their customers and to motivate their employees.

Companies whose business models are based on repeated usage need loyal customers. To attract and retain loyal customers, those companies must appeal to skilled, professional, loyal employees. To satisfy quality employees, they must respect, appreciate, and support those people who work at the company, or are interested in doing so.

The success and sustainability of your business is on trial, and talent will be the global jury.

DIGITAL TRANSFORMATION IS GLOBAL

Perhaps nowhere in the world is the necessity of loyalty clearer than in China. As the country's middle-class booms, the availability of cheap, accessible labor is rapidly diminishing, along with its competitive advantage. Wages are rising, as are the expectations of employees, and Chinese businesses are confronting challenges already familiar to businesses in other parts of the world: stagnating returns, a scarcity of engaged customers, and a lack of loyal employees.

This insight compliments a common perception of China as an economy bursting at the seams with human capital. With a population over 1.3 billion, an economy that has grown at a rate of between 6 percent and 15 percent annually since 1990, and a reputation as the leading producer of consumer goods for the wider world, China is sometimes looked upon as the world's factory. Given the immense scale, change in China means incredible opportunity.

The truth about China is both more complex than most people realize, and much more valuable as a source of learning.

There's no doubt that some countries are adopting the tenets of the digital revolution more enthusiastically and more knowledgeably than others. Equally, many governments are encouraging this change and backing it with national programs like Germany's Industry 4.0 or China's Made in China 2025. Almost any country, however, can benefit from tapping into the wellspring of data that characterizes the digital era. It's a remarkably egalitarian revolution.

The changes in our global economy are visible across the world. They're impacting companies in practically every field of human endeavor. In short, new technologies are already changing the way the world does business.

Loyalty is one of the oldest ideas in business and one of the newest. Harness it effectively, and it can make an enormous difference to the way you approach every interaction in your working life. Neglect it, and you may find that good employees and good customers are hard to find and even harder to keep.

For those who get it right, the rewards are enormous.

CHAPTER ONE

SPECIALIZATION BREEDS CHOICE

It doesn't make any sense to try and underprice Walmart on something like toothpaste. That's not what the customer is looking to in a small store anyway. Most independents are best off, I think, doing what I prided myself on doing for so many years as a storekeeper: getting out on the floor and meeting every one of the customers. Let them know how much you appreciate them, and ring that cash register yourself. That little personal touch is so important for an independent merchant, because no matter how hard Walmart tries to duplicate it—and we try awfully hard—we can't really do it.

—SAM WALTON, FOUNDER OF WALMART

Picture a small town in America in the early twentieth century. This town has a single main street where you'll find the only general store. When a customer walks into the store, the clerk greets them by name, makes inquiries about their family, and asks for feedback about the last item they purchased.

As they respond, the clerk listens with curiosity. If the customer shares a problem they're experiencing on their farm or in their kitchen, the clerk asks them questions to ascertain their needs and, if appropriate, suggests a possible solution. Where necessary, the clerk makes a note to contact the store's suppliers in case new products have recently become available.

The customer appreciates having access to so many products in one place, perhaps with the added bonus of the option to have them delivered or to purchase on store credit. Most of all, however, they appreciate the assistance of someone who appears genuinely interested in helping them and understanding their needs, as opposed to simply pitching them a product. Each employee of the store has slightly different areas of specialized knowledge, and they feel a sense of purpose because they know that they are serving their friends and neighbors.

Now, fast-forward a few decades. The town has grown.

Instead of a single general store, it's now home to several. Each one employs more people, and their individual connections with customers are weaker. Customers can no longer rely on meeting the same people every time they shop, and staff members find it harder to remember everyone who patronizes the store.

In addition, some of the new stores specialize in certain aspects of the original general store's business, from garden equipment, to bedding, to chili sauce. Suddenly, there are numerous options to choose from and, as the bonds of personal connection loosen, both employees and customers find exercising those options an increasingly tempting prospect. The changes are twofold. Not only are businesses trying to achieve greater scale, but they are also competing with other stores for the business of their customers. From the perspective of potential employees, they may also be competing to attract the brightest and most talented individuals.

Whereas previously, the general store's position at the center of the town's economy insulated it, it now increasingly looks like a relic of a bygone age. Customers may well continue shopping at the store out of habit or convenience, but their reserves of loyalty may be relatively low. When other stores nearby—or online—offer them a better deal on the same items, or provide them with options they've never known before, they may be lured into shopping elsewhere.

The same diminishment of loyalty may be true of employees, who no longer feel a personal connection with the store's owners, and don't glean the same satisfaction from serving strangers as they do from serving friends.

Charlie Munger, a long-term business partner and collaborator of Warren Buffett, says that specialization is usually the first phase of business growth.

That can mean specialization in a particular product niche, such as a bicycle shop where customers receive unparalleled personal attention and benefit from the knowledge and experience of the staff. It can mean specializing in low prices, as Walmart has done so successfully. It can even mean, as Sam Walton was so well aware, specializing in a level of service that larger chains cannot possibly emulate, and winning customer loyalty by being prepared to make special orders and deliver at short notice.

Whatever form specialization takes, it can be a highly effective strategy for business growth. As businesses occupy and explore a niche, they become better and better at meeting the needs of customers within that niche, and that allows them to locate economies of scale and grow.

FROM TOO LITTLE CHOICE TO TOO MUCH

Another facet of specialization is that it creates choice. In many parts of the developing world, and even in some rural communities in the developed world, people have relatively few choices. They don't have access to a lot of different products or services, and those they do have are often produced locally.

In a market in India, for example, it's not uncommon to see a dozen stalls selling a virtually identical selection of fruit and vegetables. It's almost impossible for them to compete on price without ultimately driving profits down, as other stalls catch on and the lower price becomes standard.

In those circumstances, the stallholder who imports specialty fruits and vegetables such as dates or figs, or who offers a level of service his peers are unwilling to match, perhaps a delivery service, instantly differentiates himself from the pack.

As a market becomes more refined, however, the distinctions become smaller. More brands emerge, and people look to individual brands to represent particular qualities. When all they want is jeans, they will happily buy the one available brand. When they have ten brands to choose from, they select more carefully depending upon the characteristics of each brand, and the degree to which those brands match their priorities.

Another way of distinguishing between emerging and developed markets is to conceive of them as building and refining markets. These terms can apply to an entire country, to an industry, or to an individual company within that industry.

In refining markets such as Hong Kong, the UK, and France, I've worked with businesses that already have a very solid business model and market share. They're looking to capitalize on the small margins of improvement available to them in order to gain an edge over their competitors. There are a lot of gains still to be made in that final 10 percent. Slight process and product improvements, slight adjustments to managerial styles, and other minor alterations can make a big difference to the overall outcomes of the business.

In China and Brazil, a lot of the businesses I have worked with are focused primarily on the first 80 to 90 percent of their activities. They need to develop their infrastructure, employ people, identify suppliers, and create products. They're building businesses, and their successful management requires a very different skill set from refining businesses.

The opportunity to purchase previously unavailable items is often a source of enormous excitement for people in developing markets. In rural China, for example, owning a pair of jeans may be seen as a luxury. Initially, at least, the *brand* of jeans is less critical to consumers in emerging markets than the opportunity to own a product that has previously been unavailable to them, and which is usually associated with prosperity.

Similarly, when prepackaged cereal first reaches a building economy, it is often a novel product. As long as they can afford to purchase it, consumers are not particularly price sensitive (there are no comparable products against which to measure it). Instead, they're attracted by the opportunity to sample something that wasn't previously available to them. Its very existence is a selling point.

As industries and businesses enter the refining phase, however, brand becomes increasingly relevant. It can be the only means of distinguishing between dozens of superficially similar offerings, and determining which of a multitude of products matches our values most closely. In a refining economy, consumers need a way to distinguish between different varieties of cereal. Some may opt for the cheapest, others for the organic variety. Still others may prefer the one with the most appealing visual identity on the package. The cereals may still be 90 percent the same, but it's the 10 percent difference that informs customer choice.

This is the point at which brand becomes crucial. Without it, consumers are left floundering around in a sea of choice, with no means of distinguishing between the options available to them. If they buy at all, it will be almost at random, with no means of justifying or repeating their decision.

When I first started at Microsoft, I was responsible for the Office brand. As part of this role, I participated in research studies around the world, especially in emerging markets. From Eastern Europe to South East Asia, I heard remarkably similar stories. Visiting Bucharest in Romania, for example, I listened to people who associated the availability of brands with their freedom of expression.

These people told me that, prior to the fall of the Berlin Wall, they didn't have brands of soap. They had soap. They had no means of exercising the freedom to choose one variety of soap over another. They perceived branding as a means of establishing a personal identity, and the simple question of determining which brand of soap was right for them took on a profound significance.

For these people, brands were indelibly associated with choice and freedom. Instead of having only one brand of soap available to them, they suddenly had the opportunity to assess their values and decide which brand was most in line with those values. It felt like a huge step forward.

Take a stroll through the average American supermarket, however, and you could be forgiven for associating the dizzying array of choices not with freedom and possibility, but with confusion and anxiety. There are so many different brands of orange juice, or eggs, or breakfast cereals, and determining the difference between them requires a lot of effort.

In modern America, specialization has reached such a peak that the typical American supermarket carries more than thirty thousand items, and those items are changing all the time. Supermarkets may add as many as twenty thousand new products per year, with a corresponding number discontinued. As a result, choice is no longer the panacea it once was. The majority of people are feeling less and less satisfied with the choices available to them, even as the *number* of choices expands rapidly.

In *The Paradox of Choice*, Barry Schwartz cites a study in which a gourmet food store offered its clientele samples of jams and jellies from a selection of either six different flavors or twenty-four different flavors. When people selected from six different flavors, they made a purchase

30 percent of the time. When they selected from twenty-four different flavors, they purchased just 3 percent of the time. The amount of choice was so overwhelming that they simply couldn't distinguish a favored flavor well enough to make a confident decision, so they walked away.

In many parts of the developed world, choice pervades every aspect of our lives. We have choices about what we study in college, where and how we work, what we watch and listen to, what we wear, what we drive, and in just about every other area of our lives.

Twenty years ago, there was a pretty good chance that we could walk into the office in the morning and discover that we had watched the same television shows as our colleagues. This shared experience was a point of social connection. Now, with hundreds of channels at our disposal, plus movies, pay-per-view, and streaming services such as Netflix and Amazon Prime, the chances are far lower. Surprisingly, this massive proliferation of choice isn't making us any happier. As the example of the jams and jellies illustrates, it is both affecting our motivation to purchase and reducing our satisfaction with the purchases we *do* make.

In his book, Schwartz describes two distinct purchasing approaches, maximizing and satisficing. Maximizers seek to procure the best of everything. If they see a shirt they like, they will seek out every valid comparison to ensure that the shirt really is the optimal purchase. Is it the highest available quality, at the best value? Satisficers, on the other hand, seek out purchases that are good enough. When they find what they desire, they are happy. They are less concerned with the possibility that they might be missing out on something better.

Herbert A. Simon, who received a Nobel Prize in Economics in 1978, theorized that researching a decision deeply enough to be certain of maximizing the outcome was so costly in terms of time, lost income potential, and emotional investment that true maximization came from adopting a satisficing strategy.

In other words, good enough is good enough. Striving for the best is so time-consuming and emotionally draining that, overall, it leads to a poorer outcome. In a world of seemingly endless choice, opting to satisfice is becoming harder to do, because there's *always* another option just around the corner, which just might be better.

WHEN BRANDS ARE STRONG, EVERYONE WINS

Do I have the best possible job? Am I living my purpose to the fullest degree? Am I eating the right things? Sleeping too much, or not enough? Are the people I see on my social media feeds making better choices than I am?

In the developed world, these questions haunt us, affecting our sense of satisfaction and motivation. A survey conducted by Gallup, initially released in 2013 and updated annually through 2017, reveals that as many as 70 percent of working Americans aren't engaged with their jobs, costing the US economy up to $500 billion per year in lost productivity.[5]

Even more concerning is the fact that disengagement can spread through an organization like a disease, infecting previously engaged employees and bringing down productivity even further. Perhaps none of us are more influenced than millennials, who have grown up in an era where choice and its constant, conspicuous display, is a ubiquitous reality. In the United States alone, more than eighty million people fall into the millennial demographic with another hundred thousand turning twenty-one every single day.

They make up 25 percent of the US workforce, and they enter adulthood with an expectation of instant communication, real-time feedback, membership of virtual communities, and with a deficit of trust in traditional media outlets. They're highly mobile, they're confident using the Internet, and they're usually very comfortable with the concept of moving for work or working remotely. All of these factors give them choices about how, where, and when they work.

The drawback is that the level of choice they encounter can be overwhelming, leading to the same sense of dissatisfaction described by Barry Schwartz. With so many available opportunities, each of which has advantages and disadvantages, it can be difficult to make and stick with a single decision.

Many people attribute the seeming flightiness of millennials to a generational character flaw, assuming that, because millennials are so mobile and willing to relocate, they're not committed or stable employees. I don't believe that's the case.

I think the extreme levels of choice millennials face present them with conundrums previous generations have never needed to confront. In a world of similarities, choice is a form of liberation. In a world of endless choices, the time and effort required to make them effectively can become a prison.

This is where brands come in. At their best, brands can be a form of shorthand, allowing us to make choices quickly, simply, and efficiently. Importantly, millennials have shown that they can be extremely loyal to brands that they respect, and to companies where they feel that their values are aligned with the company. They've also shown that they're willing to move on, very quickly, from brands and companies with which they don't feel aligned.

Many millennials have difficulty finding a company whose values they can commit to, a trend that is exacerbated by the fact that many may be still discovering their values and determining what is most important to them. In addition, they tend to be very focused on learning and development, and will quickly tire of companies that don't facilitate an expansion of their skills and experience.

As more companies recognize the validity of those needs, and begin to cater to them, I suspect we'll find that millennials constitute a huge pool of untapped talent with the potential to be very loyal.

Loyalty is as real today as it has ever been, and many people are seeking companies that they can be loyal to. Millennials are the most obvious example, but people of all ages want to be respected and appreciated by the company they work for, and feel that their work is purposeful and making a positive difference. In emerging economies, choice brings freedom. In developed economies, it can lead to confusion and frustration. Strong brands, that people feel a connection with and are willing to be loyal to, are a solution.

What brands and organizations are you loyal to? Apple? Nike? Starbucks? Is there a sports team you support or a magazine you always read? The chances are, you're loyal to those organizations not because they send you coupons in the mail, or even because you're employed by them.

Your loyalty derives from the emotions that brands or experiences evoke in you.

Sam Walton was one of the richest men in America, and Walmart is a retail empire. Yet, as the quote from his book indicates, he was well aware that the risks to Walmart's success come not from smaller stores undercutting the retail giant in price (which would usually be nearly impossible in a traditional retail context), but from giving people an experience that Walmart finds difficult to replicate.

Relationships have the power to insulate small businesses from some of the price competition they inevitably face. They have the power to influence customer behavior, because customers feel that if they go somewhere else, they won't be understood and appreciated in the same way. Those same characteristics shape the perceptions of employees, and play a key role in determining how they feel about the company they work for. In a world where both employees and customers have more choice than ever before, relationships play a crucial role in determining a company's fate.

While it's not always easy to find a job, skilled professionals in certain industries have a lot of options. Those with in-demand skills such as software development are increasingly concerned with the values of the company or companies they work with, and refuse to settle for positions that don't satisfy them.

The increasing mobility of the digital workforce only compounds this phenomenon, giving potential employees even more choice about where they work and for whom.

At the same time, social media is shifting the way we consume news and opinions, diluting the power of top-down broadcast media and amplifying the reach of networks. People endorse brands and products via social media, shaping the perceptions of their peer groups. A study by Nielsen[6] indicated that 92 percent of people trust recommendations from peers, whereas only 29 to 47 percent of people trust advertising from companies.

In a world of such phenomenal variety, brands have the

power to shortcut the anxiety of unconstrained choice and enable us to make satisfying decisions. Strong brands create and cement a sense of belonging, support the values of their employees and their customers, and reap the benefits when those people exhibit loyalty.

Increasingly, truly forward-thinking companies are also employing technology to assist us with the decision-making process, and to further improve customer satisfaction. New technologies make it easier to do what could be called "deep listening," which we'll discuss in depth in chapter seven. This involves collecting more and more data about user preferences and using that data to generate uniquely suitable recommendations. This brings the potential to relieve us of some of the pressure that comes with constantly exercising our preferences.

Those in the developed world, who have grown up with an explosion of choice, are no longer seeking more options. They're looking for a way out of the perplexing jungle of options we find ourselves faced with, and a means of being confident and satisfied with the decisions we do make.

TECHNOLOGY AND TRUST

One route out of the malaise is signposted by technology. Artificial Intelligence (AI) bots such as Siri, Alexa, and

Cortana have reached a point where they can analyze our behavior and make recommendations for us. It may not be long before we can entrust them with tasks such as purchasing groceries, because they will understand our preferences, favorite recipes, and activity levels.

Microsoft's Xbox Kinect contains sensors that are so advanced they can monitor the behavior and read the facial expressions of users, giving them the potential to assess how much they are enjoying games and movies. Did the user get up and walk away halfway through the movie? That's probably an indication that they weren't particularly immersed in it.

With sales of eight million units in its first sixty days on the market, Kinect claimed the Guinness world record as the fastest-selling consumer electronics device. As devices such as Amazon's intelligent personal assistant, Alexa, grow in popularity, and headphones such as Apple's AirPods encourage people to connect to devices at all times, the potential for the growth of AI will only continue to skyrocket. Both of the above constitute easy ways of accessing voice-activated AI bots or agents.

As we trust technology more and more, it can take a lot of the legwork out of making decisions for us, saving us time and anxiety. It can give us suggestions that are deeply personalized and feel like the best choice, without requiring us to pursue a costly maximizing strategy.

For us to invite technology so intimately into our lives, we must feel a tremendous amount of trust and loyalty towards the companies that provide us with that technology, and believe that they have our best interests at heart. In late 2016, investigators in a murder case sought to access information stored in one of these devices. Amazon, mindful of the company's intense responsibility to protect the privacy of users, initially refused to provide the data.

This is one example of the exceptional lengths that digital companies are now prepared to go to demonstrate that they handle the data they hold about us with the utmost integrity, even to the extent of defying governmental bodies. Nonetheless, it's surely only the beginning of a much larger conversation.

Another recent example is Apple's refusal to create a "backdoor" that would have allowed the FBI to access data stored on the iPhone of the San Bernardino shooter. The company was prepared to risk the legal ramifications of that decision, because they felt that the risk of losing the trust of their customers was even greater.

As the number of choices we're faced with on a daily basis

continues to mushroom, brands must become ever more protective of their integrity, because brand perception becomes all-important. If a favored brand is perceived to have failed its customers, it's often the easiest thing in the world for those customers to switch to a different one. On the other hand, people who trust a brand will willingly and happily follow that brand's guidance on which products to buy.

In a world of intense choice, recognized and trusted brands provide comfort and reassurance, easing confusion and anxiety and allowing people to feel confident that they are making good decisions. The majority of people are ready and primed to be loyal. All they need is a brand that's deserving of their loyalty, and that relates to them in a way they like.

Loyalty develops from relationships. Humans are very social creatures, and we're loyal to those with whom we have a relationship. The better, deeper, and more longstanding the relationship, the more committed we are. Product and price differentiation can be valuable strategies, but they don't create loyalty unless they're part of a larger relationship. If your business attracts customers because of a special price offer, or a new product, how will it retain those customers when the price returns to normal or the product is no longer exclusive?

The key differentiation factor is the *experience* customers have when they walk into a store, call on the phone, or even order online. The *feeling* of loyalty goes so much deeper than a particular offer. The good news is that strong branding enables businesses of any size to generate loyalty. Small businesses often have loyal customers because those customers feel valued and appreciated, and enjoy the experience of interacting with the business.

Larger businesses that succeed are the ones that find ways of giving customers an experience that they value highly at a much larger scale. In building markets, that often means creating choice where none was previously available. In refining markets, it's more likely to involve helping customers narrow and navigate the choices they are already faced with.

An example that will doubtless be familiar to most readers is Apple. Over the past two decades, Apple has been extraordinarily successful by offering customers a mere handful of distinct products. The company does not ask people to choose between dozens of iPhones all with different designs and divergent technical specifications. It invites them to choose from a relatively limited portfolio.

SPECIALIZATION FUELS GROWTH IN CHINA AND BEYOND

In China, the country's most popular e-commerce platform, Alibaba, emerged when the founder, Jack Ma, experienced limited choices and decided to change that. In the mid-1990s, Ma was working as an English translator and had the opportunity to travel to Seattle, where he accessed the Internet for the first time. Told that it was possible to buy anything he wanted online, and nursing homesickness, Ma went in search of Chinese beer.

He easily located American and German beers, but Chinese beer remained elusive. This became his "aha" moment, where he realized that Chinese supply chains were far more fragmented than those in the United States, which led him to found Alibaba.

In its early days, Alibaba connected customers with small Chinese manufacturers. Users of the site would type in the name of the product they wanted to purchase, and the site would bring up the details of companies that could produce it for them or sell it to them.

Nowadays, Alibaba is China's answer to Amazon and has expanded into other areas such as Alipay, an online payment platform. China's Global Shopping Festival falls on November 11 and is known informally as Singles' Day, roughly equivalent to Valentine's Day. In 2016, over $20 billion worth of goods were sold through Alibaba's e-commerce sites on that day. These numbers easily eclipse the $2.74 billion and $3.07 billion generated online during Black Friday and Cyber Monday sales in the United States in the same year.

Over the course of 2015, the company processed approximately $464 billion in sales, triple the number it recorded in 2012. When Alibaba went public in 2014, the company's IPO was the largest ever seen. In building economies, Alibaba and similar companies are gaining huge traction by offering choices to people who have never known them. A similar movement is underway in India, another country with an enormous population, but very localized supply chains. There, Amazon is battling for online market share with an Indian company named Flipkart. Indonesia, Africa, Brazil, and other parts of South America, are also in the throes of similar contests. Meanwhile, those in refining economies adore brands that can relieve the stress and pressure that comes with making endless choices.

Specialization is as old as human society. In *Guns, Germs and Steel*, Jared Diamond describes tribesmen in Papua New Guinea who, despite achieving a high level of civilization early in humanity's evolution, never developed advanced societies. Diamond wondered why this was so and determined that a lack of efficient protein sources prevented the Papua New Guineans from specializing.

By contrast, populations fortunate enough to find themselves in landscapes richly populated with game found that one person could hunt effectively enough to feed many. That allowed others to excuse themselves from hunting and take on different activities, such as building shelter, or making clothes.

Nowadays, specialization is the price of entry into many markets and the fuel for growth. In emerging markets, it allows businesses to offer customers choices that they may never previously have experienced, as evidenced by Alibaba and by the joy of Romanians experiencing the availability of different brands of soap for the first time. In mature or refining markets, specialization gives brands a strong identity and enables them to appeal to people, especially millennials, who are fatigued by endless choices and want to feel a sense of belonging and loyalty.

CHAPTER TWO

CURIOSITY LEADS TO UNDERSTANDING

I have no special talents. I am only passionately curious.
—ALBERT EINSTEIN

Several years ago, I gave a lecture to a packed room of MBA students in Hong Kong. The topic was transformation and technology. I shared some of the ideas presented in this book, along with some of the cool projects happening in our research division. Secretly, I was hoping that at least a few of the smartest in the room would come up to me at the end of the talk and ask how they could land an opportunity to work at Microsoft. Luckily, I didn't need to wait until the end for that kind of interest. Someone raised their hand during the talk, and asked me what was the single most important quality I looked for when making hiring decisions.

I paused to think for a moment, knowing that it's difficult to isolate one quality above all others, but the word that clearly came to me was: curiosity. This answer surprised a few people, sparking whispering and puzzled looks, so I explained further. I told the students in the room that curiosity drives innovation, and that we need people who want to learn why things are the way they are in order to drive our efforts to find new and better ways of solving problems.

Concurrently, I was thinking of another invaluable aspect of curiosity. The people who succeed at Microsoft need to be strong collaborators, capable of working well with other people. Without curiosity about what others are expressing, employees may find it hard to build effective relationships, limiting both their career development and their potential to help the company grow. Einstein's attitude of curiosity is widely credited with responsibility for the scientific breakthroughs he pioneered, but it's as applicable to relationships as it is to technological development.

THE IMPORTANCE OF LISTENING

Most of us don't listen to understand. We listen while we're waiting for our turn to speak. When we overcome that tendency, however, we discover that through listening with genuine curiosity and an open mind, people begin to trust us and open up to us. Listening creates a connection and inculcates respect.

Truly listening to another person is one of the greatest gifts we can give them. Yet, most of us exercise our listening faculties rarely, and think of listening as a crucial business tool even more seldom. In some professions, however, the ability to listen effectively is highly prized. If you've ever visited a good therapist, you've experienced the profound value of being fully and completely listened to.

Therapists are paid, essentially, to listen and to understand. They focus their attention on their clients, and when they ask questions, their intent is not to challenge or criticize but to understand their client's perspective more completely.

The best therapists find that their clients become incredibly loyal to them, and that those clients don't believe that another therapist could understand them as clearly. Occasionally, clients even fall in love with their therapists, and find it extremely difficult to handle their emotions when those feelings aren't reciprocated. That's the power of listening.

Michael P. Nichols, in *The Lost Art of Listening*, traces our adult expectations of being listened to, or not, back to the listening styles of our parents. "The listened to child is a confident child," he writes. "By the time children get to be four or five, empathy and its absence has molded their personalities in recognizable ways. A purely understood child grows up to expect others to be available and receptive. A child who is heard and appreciated has a better chance to grow up whole. The adult who is heard and appreciated is likely to continue to feel this way."

Nichols's description of empathic listening shares much with the listening style of therapists. When a child cries, a parent may respond by showing genuine care and trying to understand what has upset them, by ignoring them, by telling them to be quiet, or in a number of other ways.

Over time, children detect patterns in the way they are listened to, and adjust their expectations and their personalities accordingly. Children who are listened to consistently feel a sense of acceptance and belonging, whereas those who are not treated with empathy feel lonely and isolated.

Psychologically, the sense that those we care about aren't really listening to us is extremely painful, as is the sense that those who *have* listened to us may cease to do so. A sympathetic ear can be a powerful force in generating and cementing meaningful relationships, and its lack is the greatest barrier to creating a sense of understanding and cooperation.

While the desire to be listened to is strongest in children, we never outgrow it completely, and it applies not only to individuals, but also to brands or companies. When a brand that we care about appears not to be listening to us, it hurts, and that makes it less likely that we will trust, recommend, and purchase from that brand again in the future.

Dr. John Dewey, one of America's most profound philosophers, said, "The desire to be important is the deepest urge in human nature." This is as true in a business context as it is in a personal context. Mary Kay Ash, founder of Mary Kay Cosmetics, echoed Dewey's words, saying:

> "Make people feel valuable. Everyone has an invisible sign hanging from their neck saying, 'Make me feel important.'"

Henry Ford, most often recognized for demonstrating that

an entire car could be assembled in a mere ninety-three minutes by workers trained to specialize in individual tasks, also understood this principle, when he said, "If there is any one secret of success, it lies in the ability to get the other person's point of view, and see things from that person's angle as well as your own." While Ford made that pronouncement at a time when manufacturing was a key component of the American economy, listening has only become more important since then.

On an assembly line, each person fulfills a discrete function and can be replaced relatively easily. Some might be more or less skilled, but none are uniquely valuable. In the knowledge economy, it's vital to engage with each person's individual characteristics, and to really care about their state of mind and success. As the knowledge economy continues to grow and develop, every manager and employee will need to make listening part of their skill set.

Dale Carnegie, in his seminal *How to Make Friends and Influence People*, famously pointed out that: "You can make more friends in two months by becoming interested in other people than you can in two years by trying to get other people interested in you." In a service economy, where people grade their experiences depending upon how they feel when they interact with you, or with your company, this is even more apposite. Listening with curiosity and empathy is indispensable.

THE MANAGER AS COACH AND CHIEF LISTENER

As organizations grow in complexity and tackle more complicated problems, many good managers are finding that one of the most effective ways of relating to their employees is as a coach, listening with empathy and finding ways to get the best out of the people with whom they work.

In a world of distractions, this can be a difficult role to play. Many of us have lost the habit of concentrating our attention, and of placing the needs of the person we're listening to before our own, both of which are essential aspects of listening well. Stephen R. Covey, in *The Seven Habits of Highly Effective People*, summarizes this perfectly when he writes, "Seek first to understand, then to be understood."

Coaching is about connecting with people, inspiring them to do their best, to grow and learn, and sometimes it's about challenging them to come up with solutions on their own. Good coaches listen well, and managers who wish to coach effectively need to develop the skills of effective listening.

This is especially true in the one-on-one, a very common

format for interaction between managers and employees. Most organizations today utilize this style of interaction, whether formally or informally, to discuss progress and realign priorities. These meetings are effective only when there's a meaningful connection between manager and employee, and that connection comes from the employee's trust that they will be heard and understood.

When I'm conducting one-on-ones with team members at Microsoft, I always approach them with the intention to import anxiety and export energy, by which I mean that I look to understand the employee's worries and concerns, and give them understanding, support, encouragement, clarity and whatever resources they need to succeed.

Typically, I find that people enter these one-on-ones with frustrations and anxieties that they want to discuss. I'm happy to address those challenges and offer advice where appropriate, but it's more important to me that they leave the room energized, refocused, and ready to carry that energy to other people in the organization.

To do that, I focus primarily on what Edgar Schein called "pure inquiry." I encourage employees to lead the conversation by asking them questions such as: "Where would you like to start?" Sometimes it's necessary to set boundaries to ensure that the discussion is as productive as possible, and that it focuses on the employee's lived experience. They may be stressed about meeting upcoming targets that haven't yet been set, for example, but that's not an area they can directly influence at the time, either during the conversation or after they leave the room.

The day-to-day stresses of employees are important, naturally, but creating the space in which pure inquiry can take place often leads indirectly to much better performance, by bringing sticking points to the surface. Pure inquiry tends to drive more constructive thinking and lead to creative solutions, by helping people focus on their own situation and areas in which they can improve. It invites reflection and instills in people the belief that they can address their own challenges, rather than always relying upon their boss for solutions.

Additionally, in many business cultures, a taboo develops against speaking out once a manager has made a contribution. That can make it very hard to draw people out if I start expressing opinions before they've had an opportunity to express themselves fully.

At Microsoft, we've pioneered a structure we call "Connects," and we require managers and employees to engage in them at least two or three times per year. A Connect is a very simple written document consisting of four questions. Two of them are headed "looking backwards," and two are headed "looking forwards." The looking backwards section encourages employees to reflect on some aspects of their work that have been successful since the previous Connect, and on ways in which they feel their performance could have been better.

The looking forwards section invites employees to clarify their focus over the coming months, and to assess what help and support they will need to reach their goals for professional development.

As a manager, I spend considerable time preparing for Connects and considering my own responses. The employee and I discuss their responses, unpack some of the factors that drove those responses, and reach shared conclusions that we're both happy with, including very clear expectations, before we submit the document.

Working at a multinational company in China, a lot of employees naturally don't have English as a first language, so creating a written record is especially important when using English to communicate with one another and to document the conversation in Microsoft's global system. This also gives them something to refer to at a later date, ensuring that they understand the conversation and its outcomes. Even when employees do speak English as a first language, written answers remove ambiguity and make the process as clear and transparent as possible.

None of this is to suggest that empathy alone is sufficient. It's still important for employees to be focused and productive, and it's still important for managers to take a lead where necessary. The key is for managers to enter into conversations with the understanding that, in a complex business environment, they do not have all the answers, and that open-ended questions are a means of determining both what they don't know as well as how they can help.

In difficult situations, for example when an employee is performing poorly, listening to understand can be a lot more effective than simply reprimanding the employee. In fact, bringing performance up to standard is a key part of caring about employees and encouraging loyalty. A little tough love at the right time can prevent a negative situation from escalating and salvage a working relationship that could otherwise have ended with the employee leaving the company.

I've known managers who sought to avoid conflict and provide encouragement rather than addressing problems head-on, and then, at a later date, have wanted to terminate the employee's employment. Is that really helping the employee, who might have been able to bring their performance up to standard if they had known where they were failing to meet expectations? Is it really helping the company, which will need to invest afresh in training and integrating someone new, when the existing employee already understood the company culture, was familiar with other members of the team, and may have been largely performing well?

Employees thrive on accountability and empowerment, and part of a manager's role is giving them that, even when it includes constructive feedback to help them better achieve their targets or goals.

THE DIFFERENCE BETWEEN HEARING AND LISTENING

It's easy to think that spending time with someone constitutes listening to them, but that's not enough. For someone to truly feel that you're listening to them, they must feel that you are giving them your attention, curiosity, empathy, and desire to make a connection. They must recognize your commitment to the conversation, expressed through eye contact and body language.

Eye contact will give you insights into another person's state that might be easily missed if you were relying exclusively on verbal cues. It's easy to hear what people are saying even if you're multitasking and not giving them your full attention, but it's low-grade attention in comparison with truly listening to them. Listening is an active process.

In many modern companies, it has become acceptable to sit in a meeting with a computer or a tablet and to multitask while the meeting is going on, perhaps with several chat windows and a research document open on the desktop. While this may feel efficient, it doesn't give anyone speaking in the meeting the sense that they are being truly listened to. That's passive hearing, and if it becomes the norm, it may erode people's trust that they are being listened to and respected.

By contrast, if someone sits across from me, shuts their computer, and engages with me using eye contact and open body language, I'll truly feel that they are seeking to understand me, which will lead to a sense that they respect me. It's a very positive experience, and I'll probably walk away from it feeling understood.

Company-wide, failing to listen effectively can manifest in an approach that privileges policy over connection. Perhaps you've called a customer helpline with a complaint or a concern, only to be told that the company's policy doesn't allow them to serve you effectively. It's a deeply frustrating experience, and it almost certainly doesn't improve your perceptions of the company in question.

It's very common for companies to coach people on their speaking skills, but very few offer training in listening. Most people believe that they already listen well. To test your listening skills, imagine this scenario. You're commencing a meeting, and one of the attendees walks in late. They've done it before. How do you respond? Do you make a comment about their lateness? Do you ignore it? Do you take them aside after the meeting and ask them whether they are OK?

If you choose the third option, and continue to exercise your curiosity and ask further questions, you may discover that they have problems at home that make it hard for them to show up on time for that meeting slot. You may be able to find a solution, perhaps by changing the time of the meeting.

An effective formula is to share an observation, follow that up with a statement about the impact the behavior is having, and express curiosity. So, in the example above, the observation could be: "I noticed that you came into this morning's meeting late." Notice that the observation doesn't imply judgment or criticism. It's simply a statement about what is.

The impact of the behavior might be that the employee is missing key information, or that there's a risk other members of staff perceive them negatively. Curiosity invites them to share their experience, by saying: "Help me understand."

Once both parties are confident that understanding has been reached, it's time to move towards a resolution. As a manager, your objective here is to find a way of moving forward together.

Some people confuse resolution and discipline. "OK," they think, "now I understand why you were late. Be on time next time." Resolutions are based on what you have heard and discussed. If your team member has another commitment that clashes with the start of a meeting, maybe it's possible to shift the meeting time, or set an expectation with the rest of the team that allows for late arrival. If they have experienced a family emergency, you can reassure them that it's OK, and ask them to let you know the next time it happens.

This feedback process is a difficult skill to master, because it requires that you suspend your judgment of an employee's behavior in order to truly understand their experience. It will succeed only if you resist the temptation to presume that you know what they are thinking and feeling. Hearing someone passively will never suffice in this scenario. It requires full engagement and a curious mindset.

When you do this, you may learn totally unexpected things about your employees, and put yourself in a position to manage them much more effectively, while simultaneously gaining their trust and loyalty.

Nonetheless, being open and empathetic can be nerve-wracking for the listener, because when you access genuine curiosity, you don't know what you'll hear. It involves giving up control. Being on the other side of the interaction can also be extremely challenging. Many people are unused to receiving empathetic listening. When given the compassionate ear of a superior, they may find previously buried emotions rising to the surface.

Brené Brown, a researcher on shame and vulnerability at the University of Houston, writes that shame is: "The intensely painful experience of believing that we are unworthy of love and belonging. Empathy is the antidote to shame." When we listen to people with empathy and curiosity, either in a personal or a professional context, their fears that they are unworthy of love and belonging may make themselves known.

This is particularly true in Asia, where shame is an especially powerful emotion. Handling situations where shame is involved requires even more empathy, and it can take considerable patience before a person really trusts that they will be listened to.

Empathy is not the end of the conversation. It's the beginning. Personal difficulties are not an excuse for poor performance, and it's perfectly acceptable to combine empathy with high standards and expectations that employees will make a course correction where necessary. When used effectively, however, curiosity and non-judgmental listening conveys respect. Employees who feel that they are respected will be more engaged, and ultimately more loyal, than those who do not.

IF I LEAVE, OTHERS WON'T KNOW ME AS WELL

A manager who listens effectively plays a key role in retaining quality employees. People stay at companies where they feel known and understood, particularly by their manager.

If a good manager leaves for another company, it's possible that others will follow, because they know that manager understands them. The reverse is true of a poor manager; one who doesn't listen effectively. When a poor manager is in charge, employee retention rates may dip significantly, and job satisfaction will tumble.

There's a tangible benefit to being the kind of manager who takes the time to listen proactively to employees, understands their strengths, preferences, and challenges, and gets the best out of them. Not only will they be much more likely to stay with the company, the trust that comes with understanding will free them to take creative risks and give their best work.

Listening to employees is a form of investment. It's a commitment of time and energy that pays dividends over the long haul. The more "equity" there is in the relationship, the more trust and loyalty is available. No one wants to see their investments fail, and once we've invested successfully in a relationship, we're motivated to continue investing further. That's true of a spousal relationship, of a connection with a doctor, a manager, and even an entire brand.

When a relationship has a lot of built-up equity, the occasional mistake is easily tolerated and forgiven. The overall experience of the relationship is strong and positive, so minor blips cause minimal concern. The opposite is true of a relationship that lacks equity. Mistakes and disappointments take on greater significance, and the desire to end the relationship entirely can become very strong.

We trust people who take the time to listen to us and

understand us, because we believe that they have our best interests at heart.

There was a time, during the heyday of manufacturing, when it was relatively easy to neglect listening skills in the workplace. Strength and self-reliance were highly prized, and empathetic listening was a comparatively low priority. As service industries gain traction, however, and increasing numbers of us find that our business success relies upon our capacity to create, sustain, and develop trusting relationships, listening skills are no longer optional. If we want happy, engaged employees, they are compulsory.

LISTENING TO CUSTOMERS AND CLIENTS

Bill Gates famously commented that, "Your most unhappy customers are your greatest source of learning." As a business leader, there are few times I learn more about what's really happening than when I sit down and deeply listen to customers and the questions they have. The more engaged they are, and often the more they challenge me or my company, the more I learn. Similarly, managers who listen effectively to employees will convey that habit through the company, leading to a better standard of listening when employees are in conversation with customers. This could not be more important.

Whatever channel employees are using to connect with customers, whether in person, on the phone, on Twitter or Facebook, or via some other medium, it's essential that they listen effectively, either to solve customers' problems, or at least to allow them to feel understood. In person, body language and eye contact are vital. In any circumstance, customers need the full attention and engagement of employees if they are to feel understood and respected.

Sales conversations are not about trying to convince people to buy. They're about understanding what the customer needs and wants and what challenges they're experiencing in their business. From that platform of trust, suggesting solutions becomes a natural progression. A good salesperson understands their client's needs, and strives to assist them in solving business problems. If they are successful, the client naturally *wants* to buy. No coercion is required.

This type of listening dialogue can become a habit, so that every conversation with the client takes the form of genuinely inquiring into their business needs and, where possible, meeting those needs. Instead of becoming a high-pressure ordeal for both the salesperson and the client, sales conversations can become an opportunity for mutual trust and understanding to develop.

If customer service is a ladder, feeling listened to lies approximately halfway up. When customers feel listened to, they invite the possibility of climbing the ladder further. Solve their problems in a way they appreciate, and they'll be satisfied. Satisfy them repeatedly, and they'll become loyal.

Your success will come in direct proportion to your open-mindedness and curiosity. It's easy to think that successful selling consists of selling a product. It would be more accurate to say that it's about selling a feeling, and cultivating that feeling can be more valuable than delivering functionality.

Ralph Waldo Emerson said, "Every man I meet is in some way my superior." It's a perfect description of a listening mindset. We can learn something from everyone we meet. It's important not only to understand a client's needs, but also to make sure that *they* know you've heard their needs, seek to meet those needs, and finally confirm that you've delivered on your promise and that they perceive you to have delivered on your promise.

Both internally and externally, this listening mindset represents a considerable shift from a traditional top-down approach. Take the example of giving a presentation. In days gone by, it would be common to outline an agenda, fulfill that agenda and, if feedback was called for, hand out a survey asking whether the presentation covered the promised material. This is especially common in the case of talks delivered to large audiences.

The more modern way is to ask participants what's on their mind and what challenges they're facing, and then to adapt the presentation to meet those needs. When speaking to a large audience, this is difficult to do, but engaging with people before and after giving a speech, and listening attentively to other speakers, can convey a mindset of curiosity. This approach requires a lot more spontaneity and responsiveness, but it has the potential to be much more rewarding for everyone involved.

When a presentation is delivered in this fashion, the primary metric of success becomes not whether all the anticipated material is covered, but whether it resolves the challenges participants offer up to be discussed. The traditional presentation is analogous to broadcast media, while the modern presentation is analogous to social media. The former tells people what the presenter deems that they need to know. The latter adopts a listening mindset and aims to respond effectively to their needs.

Real Madrid, one of the greatest soccer clubs in the world, has a passionate global fan base of more than 450 million people. Until recently, however, the club lacked a method of engaging directly with that fan base.

Leaders at the club felt that it was critical for them to connect more effectively with their fans, and to learn from them, because ultimately the club belongs to them. To do this, they embarked upon a digital transformation initiative. In conjunction with consultants and technological partners, the club created a fan engagement platform that aggregated data from social media outlets and monitored what people were saying about Real Madrid.

Fans were given the opportunity to complete online fan profiles at the club's official website, and to search an archive of video footage so they could replay their favorite moments of games. A new app allowed fans to gain virtual access to the Bernabéu, Real's stadium, before, during, and after each game. A database of the club's players offered fans the opportunity to learn everything they wanted to know about their heroes.

Excitingly, they were able to analyze this data using cloud computing services and understand how fans were engaging with the suite of products they had created, measuring sentiment and even predicting what they might do next.

This gave Real tremendously valuable insights into the

sentiments and states of mind of their fans, allowing the club to provide them with a better experience, market merchandise more effectively, and assess how positive or negative they felt. I spoke recently at a large event for Euro League, a brand that was holding a conference to discuss expansion into China. This topic sparked more audience interest than any other.

MasterCard, at the company's headquarters in New York, has found another way of listening. Situated in a large, open plan office is an area known as Insights Alley, containing a lounge with casual seating and fifty-five screens broadcasting trending news stories. The screens also monitor feeds and performance metrics for more than sixty markets in which MasterCard has a stake, and real-time data relating to the effectiveness of campaigns.

Insights Alley was created in 2012 with the intention of bringing all the data that would otherwise be found in disparate reports to a single hub. The information it provides is instrumental in making decisions about marketing spend and slogans, and increases the company's ability to respond quickly to trends and current events.

During the 2015 Rugby World Cup, it became clear that the company's Apple Pay promotions were reaching more people via social media than the web. Taking advantage of this information, the company was able to adjust the campaign in real time.

Insights Alley is a fairly casual space, and anyone in the office can use it as they see fit. A product manager who has just launched a new campaign might take their laptop there and watch as the results are transmitted. During a major news event, people might gather there and assess the impact on the business. At all times, Insights Alley remains a resource to be drawn from and a digital method of keeping an ear to the ground.

NONVERBAL LISTENING

In 2009, I lived and worked in Brazil. I was the first employee of Microsoft in Brazil who didn't speak Portuguese. When the team originally proposed that I consider the move, it seemed a bit crazy—and a little intimidating—to contemplate living and working in an environment where I couldn't understand what people were saying.

Brazil is a very large country, and at first, I found it very difficult. At the time, the majority of Brazilians, both within Microsoft and more generally, didn't speak much better English than I spoke Portuguese. Although I started learning Portuguese, I had to find a way of conducting myself in a business environment long before I attained any level of fluency. Often, people would switch to English when I was in the room, even if their skills were limited, and switch back to Portuguese the instant I left. I still remember feeling hesitant to even step out of meetings and use the restroom, because everyone would notice that I had left and would quickly switch their language.

Despite my limited Portuguese, I found that I was able to quickly pick up body language and facial expressions that reflected the culture. By focusing on communicating through physical gestures and facial expressions, I was able to establish a rapport even with people I didn't share a common language with. This was especially effective in Brazil, where there's a very expressive physical culture. For almost the entire first year I was in Brazil, I communicated primarily by reading people's body language and responding appropriately.

Incredibly, customers and employees felt that I understood them, and I felt that way, too. Even while my Portuguese was very limited, I was able to use one or two words, expressed in the drawn-out Portuguese style, and people were impressed that I was learning the language. They complimented me on my Portuguese, even though in reality I knew very little.

Now that I'm living and working in China, many people

think that I speak Chinese. I'm learning the language, but my level is still quite basic. Instead, I rely on picking up on subtle physical and facial gestures. By reading nonverbal cues, I find that I can often understand people despite the lack of a shared language. They feel understood. More importantly, because I am trying my hardest to listen both to their spoken and unspoken expressions, they know that I care.

CHAPTER THREE

RESPECT BUILDS TRUST

The more vulnerable we can be with one another, the more that we'll trust one another, and the more we'll be able to collaborate effectively.

—NEIL BLUMENTHAL, CO-FOUNDER
AND CO-CEO OF WARBY PARKER

Every year at Microsoft we survey employee sentiment. As part of the survey, employees are asked to choose one word to describe different aspects of life on the team. Consistently, the one word I see emerging from members of my team is "trust."

Perhaps because of this, other managers at Microsoft

often approach me to ask for advice on building trust within their teams. Usually, I respond by asking them about the levels of respect in those teams. In most cases, they reply quickly that of course their team members respect them. They are the managers, and therefore the senior figures in charge—a dynamic that is especially pronounced in Asia. At this point, I clarify that my question is not about whether the manager feels respected. It is about whether the individuals on their team feel that the manager respects *them*.

Often, that's a lightbulb moment for managers. They recognize the shift I'm asking them to make, and they pause to ask themselves honestly whether their team members feel respected.

Respect is a basic component of trust. It's nearly impossible to build a trusting relationship with someone if they feel that you don't respect what they say, how they feel, or even the way they look. On the other hand, respect opens doors to new insights. Everyone has something to share if you respect them enough to listen.

This need for respect is so universal that it even transcends the species barrier, as you can prove for yourself when interacting with animals. The next time you meet a pet, kneel down to their level, give them space, and let them approach you and begin to sniff you before you reach out to pet them. You may be much bigger and stronger than they are, but if you wish to win their trust, it's important that you place yourself on an equal footing with them.

For the same reason, it's OK as a manager to admit to fears and mistakes. These sophisticated expressions of vulnerability are part of what makes us human. Used skillfully, they have a role to play in breaking down the barriers of status encouraging employees to share their own challenges and anxieties.

Respect is the positive feeling of being understood, and it starts with good listening. The quality of relationships between employees, and of their interactions with customers, has a more profound impact on loyalty levels than the price of products. In an office situation, managers may receive basic respect due to their position, even if they don't treat their employees especially well.

Similarly, customers may tolerate a lack of respect if they are in a hurry or they need a product that is difficult to find elsewhere. It may only be outside these scenarios that they begin to talk, telling others whether they love their job, or whether they love the service they receive from a particular company.

What's the opposite of respect? In the bestselling *Blink*, Malcolm Gladwell relates the perspective of relationship expert, John Gottman. Gottman has researched marriage for more than forty years, and couples attending his workshops relapse into negative habits only half as often as those who experience standard therapy. His book, *The Seven Principles for Making Marriage Work*, is rich with insight and information.

Gottman can observe a couple for five minutes and determine, with 91 percent accuracy, whether they will divorce. As Gladwell explains it:

> "If Gottman observes one or both partners in a marriage showing contempt toward the other, he considers it the most important sign that the marriage is in trouble."

In an intimate relationship, contempt dissolves the bonds of trust and appreciation like acid, eroding everything that ever made the participants compatible. Gottman believes that if even one person in a marriage treats the other with contempt, the union is doomed to almost certain failure. By contrast, couples that respect one another attain far better marital outcomes, because each person feels that their partner understands and supports them.

How we feel in the presence of another person is a key

factor in determining whether we love them, hate them, or somewhere in between. Without the belief that they respect us, it's very difficult to feel positive towards them. As it is in our personal lives, so it is in our working lives. Without respect, it's virtually impossible to build trust and, with that trust, functioning, positive relationships.

Listening with curiosity, as outlined in the previous chapter, is essential to the cultivation of respect. An equally important component, which we'll discuss in this chapter, is a commitment to valuing and encouraging the contributions of others.

Derek Sivers, in a YouTube video that has garnered more than four million hits to date, highlights the importance of a leader respecting their first one or two followers.[7] The video shows a "lone nut," as Sivers describes him, dancing in a field at what appears to be a music festival. Groups of people are dotted around the field, largely ignoring him.

The tone changes when another person joins the action. This "first follower" legitimizes the first guy's activities, and the leader takes the opportunity to welcome him in turn. Before long, a third person joins the fray, swiftly followed by several others. All of a sudden, a movement is born, and it is those *not* dancing who look out of place.

When people feel respected, they open up and dare to share themselves in ways they otherwise wouldn't. As the video illustrates so clearly and humorously, people who see a leader treating their first followers as equals feel safe to add their voices, or their bodies, and make a contribution, trusting that it will be valued and appreciated. Anyone who leads must inevitably contend with the fear, and sometimes the reality, of ridicule. What Sivers makes clear, however, is that the way a leader behaves towards their first followers defines a movement, or a business.

Whenever I find myself in the role of leader, especially in the context of driving transformation, one of my key roles is to encourage the first followers to speak up. This is especially true in Asia, where shyness towards authority figures is culturally prevalent, and people often require considerable encouragement before they summon the courage to speak up in a group situation.

Generally speaking, if I ask a new team to share ideas and opinions about a project, the room will be very quiet for a minute or two before anyone speaks up. When a member of the team breaks the silence, I *always* offer them positive feedback, simply for making a contribution. At that stage, the quality of the contribution is less important than conveying the sense that their efforts are valued. Over time, the message spreads through the group, unlocking input that might otherwise have remained unexpressed.

When a group meets regularly, and each person finds that their ideas are respected, the overall atmosphere of the group gradually grows more comfortable and relaxed, and people feel comfortable sharing ideas that they would have kept to themselves in more tense situations.

The same is true in large presentations, where I always seek to validate questions from the audience. If, as a presenter, I gave people the impression that their questions and ideas were stupid, I would soon find that they stopped asking questions and sharing ideas. That's the exact opposite of what I want to accomplish.

When you're trying to drive change within an organization, by definition you're asking people to step out of their accustomed roles and do things they haven't done before. To do that, they need to feel safe. For example, a few years ago, I was heading a team responsible for organizing a large annual event in collaboration with Microsoft's partner community in Hong Kong.

That community consisted of more than two thousand partner companies, and we were accustomed to running it at a large, expensive convention center, one of the few venues in Hong Kong big enough to hold representatives of all the companies.

At the time, our business was transforming in some very significant ways, and we wanted the conference to reflect the shifts Microsoft was going through. We wanted to send a message to our partners that Microsoft was changing, and that would reflect the way we chose to do business with them, and also that it was incumbent upon them to transform *their* approaches to doing business with us.

Initially, brainstorming sessions for the conference were quite challenging. At the time, I was quite new to the team, and the embedded culture didn't involve a lot of creative thinking. As a result, members of the team took a lot of encouragement before they were willing to contribute. Eventually, however, new ideas began to flow. One person suggested structuring the agenda differently and inviting some unexpected speakers.

I made a point of offering a lot of positive feedback and reassurance, to give the impression that person's contribution was very valuable. Which it was: Speaking up when no one else was willing opened the door to other people to voice their ideas.

Finally, I invited the quietest person on the team to speak

up. She was very introverted, and convincing her to open up required a large investment of trust on my part, and a willingness to create an environment in which she knew her input would be appreciated. When she spoke, it was to suggest that we change the venue of the conference from the traditional conference center to a modern art museum called the Asia Society, to reflect the ways in which Microsoft was changing as a company and to engage our partners' attention in a new way.

We scaled down the list of invitees and, by situating the conference in a modern, artsy venue, it gave a clear signal to our partners about the changes at the company with one simple move.

The conference was a huge success. When our partners completed their feedback forms, they told us the way we altered the venue, and made the agenda much more fun, engaging, and concise, really conveyed the message that Microsoft was becoming a much more approachable, open-minded company. That wouldn't have been possible without the quietest, most introverted member of our leadership team receiving the message that her contributions were to be valued.

People who are considering expressing themselves in a group tend to feel extremely vulnerable. They fear that by sharing openly they are opening themselves up to ridicule and embarrassment. As a leader, I now see embodying, embracing, and encouraging vulnerability as an essential part of running an effective group. A leader who expresses vulnerability allows other members of the group to do the same, and when their efforts are respected, they present ideas and solutions that might otherwise never have been suggested.

There's a Portuguese expression that translates loosely as: "Whatever happens in the kitchen is fine, but when the food is served, we must all be in agreement." It means that debate and discussion are welcomed, as long as every member of the team is pulling together when the time comes to deliver. Mutual respect allows this to become a reality, by creating a space in which ideas and opinions can be safely shared, with every person's input welcomed as a contribution to a greater whole.

PRINCIPLE OVER POLICY

Respect can be hard to come by. It takes time and sincere effort to cultivate, and it can be easily lost with a careless word or an unkind gesture.

In a "top-down" culture, respect is at less of a premium. The powerful figures within those cultures have a license to dictate terms to employees, and their words are law. They command respect by means of their positions. Another example is the military, traditionally an organization with a clearly defined chain of command, to the extent that disobeying the order of a superior can lead to a court-martial.

Even the military, however, is beginning to change. Around the world, many combat forces are becoming more agile, more distributed. A special operations team, operating behind enemy lines in a volatile environment, will probably not be able to rely on constantly receiving instructions from a distant command center. Instead, members of that team will need to make decisions on their own as the situation in which they find themselves changes.

It's a vulnerable position to be in, and one in which it's hard to know exactly what the right thing to do is. To operate successfully, members of the team must work together and have tremendous trust and respect for each other. They must also understand the principles behind their mission, in case the field situation changes and they need to adjust. This enables them to make the best possible decisions on the field of battle.

As a counterpoint, consider the legal system in the United States. The potential to be sued is so great that many people and many companies are terrified to admit to any degree of vulnerability. If there's a chance that they're wrong, there's also a chance that they could find themselves on the wrong end of a court case. In those circumstances, people and organizations are naturally reticent to say anything that could be held against them. Any expression of fault may lead to legal liability.

It's sometimes very difficult to give or receive respect in a culture with such a high risk of legal action. In a business culture, it can have an effect not only on the willingness of individuals to open up in a group setting, but also on the way the company presents itself to customers and clients.

One way in which this manifests is an adherence to policy over principle. Have you ever called a customer helpline seeking some kind of support, and been told that the agent can't help you because whatever situation you're facing is not covered by company policy?

If so, how did you feel? Frustrated? Annoyed? Probably you felt that your concerns were not being heard, understood, or respected, and when you hung up the phone, you were left with a negative impression of the company.

Now imagine instead of being told that policy trumps principle, you were told that principle trumps policy. When you call, the agent on the other end of the phone will treat you with respect *because it's the right thing to do*. They will try to resolve your problem, *because it's the right thing to do*. And if they don't succeed, they will at least reassure you that they take your concerns seriously and will take steps to pass your query on to the relevant department or manager.

In short, they will engage with you as a fellow human being rather than hiding behind the wall of policy. How would you feel after hanging up after that phone call, even if your troubles weren't immediately resolved?

Nowadays, the Hilton hotel is one of the most famous names in hospitality in the world. Years ago, however, one of the earliest Hilton hotels opened in Chicago. It was known as the Palmer House. As the hotel became more popular, the staff found that they were turning away more and more guests because the hotel was full. Sometimes this happened late at night, and guests didn't know where else to go.

The *policy*, in that situation, was to tell potential guests that the hotel was full and turn them away. The *principle*, however, was to make guests feel as comfortable as though they were in their own home. This principle drove numerous innovations.

A hotel desk was created with the specific agenda of finding rooms at other, nearby hotels for people who arrived while the hotel was full. The hotel management also set up a room where people who arrived before their room was ready could take a shower and freshen up. Adhering strictly to policy would have seen the hotel simply telling people they couldn't help. Acting out of principle resulted in a clientele that felt special, important, and cared for whenever they set foot in a Hilton hotel.

In another industry, and with employees the beneficiaries as opposed to customers, FedEx gave its managers the power to reward those who had done a particularly good job with something they knew that employee would particularly appreciate.

These were not standard performance-based incentives. They were more about recognizing those times when employees went above and beyond the call of duty to give the customer great service, with gifts that were uniquely valuable, such as tickets to a specific theater performance or to the sporting event of a favorite team. The gifts were designed to be personalized to the employee's particular preferences, so that they felt rewarded, understood, and yes, respected by their managers and by the company as a whole.

FedEx could have created a policy that rewarded good

service with standard bonuses. By operating, instead, from the principle that people value gifts that are tailored to their specific interests and preferences, they did much more.

EMBRACING VULNERABILITY TO ENCOURAGE INNOVATION

As more businesses understand the value of treating both employees and clients with respect, new business models are emerging that simply wouldn't have been possible in a top-down environment.

Consider Kickstarter, where people with potential new businesses invite would-be patrons to preorder their products, funding their manufacture. Kickstarter would have been unthinkable in an environment where the founders and executives of a company were determined to project the appearance of always knowing what was right. Its very existence depends upon the willingness of entrepreneurs to open their ideas up to scrutiny, and sink or swim based on the response of potential customers.

When they receive enough support from people who believe in their ideas, entrepreneurs using Kickstarter can continue to develop their businesses and expand into other markets.

Cards Against Humanity, billing itself as "a party game for horrible people," is an example of a product that has thrived through Kickstarter. The game's inventors took a chance that other people shared their sense of humor and launched via the platform. It quickly became clear that there was a significant market for the game, and it has subsequently become very successful.

Another way in which creators can showcase their work is to sell through an online marketplace such as Etsy. Potentially, this allows them to reach a far larger audience than they could have done without going online, although it also requires them to handle the vulnerability of exhibiting their creations to everyone on the Internet.

The same logic can be true at larger, more established companies, where it's sometimes possible for a small segment of a company to become a laboratory for testing out ideas and innovations. At Microsoft, for example, we've made a big cultural shift in terms of how we measure performance and compensate our engineers.

Previously, engineers would program features that they thought were valuable, and we would ship them. Now, we have a model where we can monitor, in an aggregated fashion, the usage of features that our engineers create. This allows us to take general measurements of what people are clicking on and using, in real time. This approach gives us a clearer idea than we've ever previously had of which features are proving popular, and it also allows us to request feedback to improve them.

Again, the software engineers have the opportunity to make a unique contribution to the experience of users of Microsoft products. They can make a real and tangible difference in the lives of millions of people. There's also a risk that they will labor on perfecting a particular feature, only to find that it isn't well received.

In the digital era, testing out ideas is easier and cheaper than ever before, and a willingness on the part of companies and individuals to share their work, even when it seems imperfect or unfinished, is driving a change in culture. The founders of Tesla, a very innovative force in the automotive industry, have pioneered this approach by open-sourcing their engineering plans. Their justification is that they want to make the world a better place, so if they have good ideas, they want other people to be able to use them and build on them.

Linux and Wikipedia work entirely on the principle of collaboration, allowing people from all over the world to contribute to their products, and it's common practice for Google to launch new products in beta mode, inviting feedback that can be used to improve the quality of the product.

All of these approaches are forms of listening. They say to users that their contribution is valued and needed, and that it will be treated with respect when it arrives. They also say that the company is willing to acknowledge areas in which it can do better.

The latter is a vulnerable message to send, and the former encourages users to reciprocate by sharing their own vulnerable thoughts. It's easy to shy away from such open approaches, and yet, as the examples above illustrate, some of the companies modeling and welcoming vulnerability are achieving far greater growth than organizations that retain a rigid, top-down hierarchy.

DEFINING INHERITED AND EARNED RESPECT

In some cultures, respect is based upon seniority. It's assumed that, because a person occupies a particular position, or has reached a certain age, that they are worthy of respect. Earned respect, however, is a function of actual interactions. It flows from how people treat us, and how we treat them, irrespective of our respective positions in a hierarchy.

Inherited or presumed respect often centers on ritualistic deferment, and requires those who are younger or less senior in position to treat the contributions of their elders with exaggerated politeness. Earned respect is purely behavioral. Have you ever had a boss who you felt obliged to treat politely to his or her face, but secretly found insufferable? That's the contrast between presumed respect and (a lack of) earned respect.

It's entirely possible for the two styles of respect to coexist, and they often do. When earned respect is lacking, however, relationships between managers and employees will suffer, lowering the morale of teams and impacting loyalty.

Often, the gestures that cultivate respect are small and easily overlooked. Those who respond to e-mails, for example, and ensure that they are on time for group and one-on-one meetings, actively demonstrate that they care about the experience of their peers. This is another reason why tackling behaviors such as not showing up on time to meetings, albeit with curiosity and understanding, is so important. When a tendency to be tardy is allowed to become commonplace, the entire group receives a message that their time is not respected.

Many managers are shocked by this distinction. They imagine that their employees undoubtedly respect them.

As described at the opening of this chapter, however, the deeper question is whether the manager respects their employees. I've conducted exit interviews with the intention of discovering why an employee has left the company, and discovered that they didn't feel heard or understood by their manager. People complain that their ideas are dismissed, and their manager assumes that he or she knows better, simply by dint of being the boss.

In an economy where skilled employees increasingly have choice and mobility, and where loyal, talented people are a scarce resource, those people will simply leave a company in which they don't feel respected. Assumed respect won't be enough to keep them. Only earned respect will suffice.

BRAND POWER

What do you think was the number one social media network in 2006? Facebook? Actually, Facebook was third, right behind MySpace and Classmates.com. So how has Facebook grown to become a global behemoth, while MySpace and Classmates.com have sunk without a trace?

One clue comes from the response of Facebook's founder, Mark Zuckerberg, to the unrest of the site's users when the site launched the feature that ultimately evolved into what we now know as the Facebook News Feed. The change brought such dissatisfaction that a petition was started requesting that it was reversed, and a call went out to boycott the site for a day. In a matter of days, the petition gathered seventy thousand signatures.

Initially, Facebook ignored the rumblings of discontent, claiming that only a few of the site's users were upset by the changes, and that the new layout was only a test. As dissent became more palpable, however, Mark Zuckerberg realized that dismissing it would be a significant mistake. He posted a very open message to the site's members, admitting that the company had really messed up the rollout of the new features, and expressing his contrition.

"We did a bad job of explaining what the new features were," he wrote, "and an even worse job of giving you control of them. That was a big mistake on our part, and I'm sorry for it."

Facebook went on to change their privacy controls to give members more control over what they made visible to others, and to continually invite user feedback as the site developed. By expressing vulnerability and making changes in line with their members' desires, they arrested the displeasure of the site's users and turned what could have been a public relations disaster into a success.

Facebook continues to listen to the feedback of users. During and immediately following the 2016 presidential election in the United States, the issue of "fake news" generated a lot of controversy. Facebook subsequently pledged to take steps to tackle the proliferation of fake news via its platform. As I write this, in 2017, Facebook is the world's largest social media network. MySpace and Classmates.com are so far behind that they barely register.

Facebook is a global brand, recognizable in almost every country in the world, and people associate that brand with openness and connectivity. Nowadays, the characteristics of particular brands, indeed the emotions that people associate with them, play an enormous role in defining the way they are perceived.

Originally, branding was a way of marking cattle, to proclaim that they belonged to their owner and ward off anyone who might be thinking of rustling them. As the marketplace has become more complex, branding has evolved to reflect those complexities.

In the 1890s, mail-order catalogs in the United States were sometimes known as wish books. They presented opportunities to aspiring people who wanted the goods they offered, and for the first time, the things they offered could conceivably be considered lifestyle brands, items that sprung not from a practical need, but from a culture of desire.

By the 1920s, factories that had produced armaments during the First World War were being repurposed to develop consumer goods on a large scale. Before long, people found themselves desiring goods they hadn't even imagined forty years previously. Around the 1940s, levels of choice had risen to a point where consumers needed assistance to help them differentiate between superficially similar products, leading to the advent of the modern brand.

IBM was one of the first companies to recognize the power that brands have to convey what a company stands for, with their THINK campaign: "I THINK, therefore IBM." Instead of denoting ownership, brands began to take on the role of communicating the essence of their parent company. Apple's "Think different" campaign could be seen as a direct successor to IBM's, positioning the company as fresh, original, and slightly outside the mainstream.

Strong brands generate emotion. The strongest create a sense of belonging in their followers. Emotion is the shortest route to a decision, and brands that spark instant recognition and positive emotions give themselves a huge advantage over those that don't.

WARBY PARKER'S INDIVIDUALITY AND QUIRKINESS

Warby Parker is a young, upstart eyeglass company based in New York. Over the past decade, Warby Parker has developed a reputation for challenging the status quo and taking a quirky, innovative approach to their business operations. The company places a premium on trust, respect, and inviting employees to express themselves vulnerably.

Warby Parker's core business is providing low-cost eyewear, mainly distributed online, but it's their brand identity and corporate culture that makes the company noteworthy. Some of Warby Parker's stores are decorated like bookstores, to highlight the connection between reading glasses and books. They run in-store events inviting people to take selfies or photographs of themselves trying on glasses.

Each pair of glasses purchased from Warby Parker, either in-store or online, generates funding for the nonprofit arm of the business, supplying glasses to someone in the developing world who otherwise wouldn't be able to afford them. Each Monday, in Warby Parker staff meetings, new employees are asked to stand up and share a fun fact or a funny story about themselves. It's a vulnerable moment, and deliberately so. The company wants to foster the perception that being a bit odd, and a bit quirky, is acceptable and encouraged.

By asking employees to embrace the experience of vulnerability during their very first staff meeting, and rewarding them with acceptance when they do, Warby Parker is cultivating comfort with the experience of speaking up. Doing this instills vulnerability as a cultural principle, and sends a clear message that the courage to be vulnerable will be respected.

Through expressing vulnerability and receiving the vulnerability of others, people earn trust and build connections. The more vulnerable they are with each other, the more they trust one another and learn to collaborate effectively. Every Wednesday, the entire team comes together to share updates from every department. Originally, the company saw this as an opportunity to understand the state of the company as a whole, but it has the added advantage of providing a learning opportunity and driving engagement.

Warby Parker conducts 360° reviews, a time-consuming, but valuable process. Each week, managers ask every employee to rate their happiness on a scale of zero to ten, potentially sparking a conversation about what needs to happen for those numbers to increase. The company also asks everyone for an idea about how they can innovate each week, stimulating employees to think about what could be done better and more effectively.

When hiring, interviewers seek to truly understand the personality of interviewees, so they ask unusual questions, such as, "What's a costume you wore in the last four weeks?" The purpose of the question is not to rule out anyone who hasn't worn a costume during the past four weeks. It's to get a sense of how interviewees respond to being asked that question. Do they take themselves seriously and find the question difficult to engage with, or do they embrace it? It's a way of assessing emotional intelligence and charisma, which they feel are important indicators of leadership potential.

ZAPPOS AND A CULTURE OF TOGETHERNESS

Another brand making bold moves in consciously promoting a unique company culture and respecting employees is the online shoe retailer, Zappos. Founded in 1999, Zappos was purchased by Amazon in 2009, but continues to operate independently. The company has created a corporate culture defined by ten core values, such as "deliver WOW," and "be adventurous." The company takes specific actions every day to reinforce the messages that Zappos is a fun place to work, and that it's also a little weird. New employees absorb these values and learn what's expected of them, with trainers always available for anyone who has questions.

The Zappos hiring process is more like a courtship than a

traditional recruitment, with HR managers often meeting potential employees in informal settings and spending considerable time with them before they agree to a relationship. The company expends a lot of energy determining whether potential employees will be a cultural fit. They conduct two interviews, one based on traditional hiring criteria, and the second oriented towards behavioral questions.

Zappos doesn't hire temporary employees during busy seasons, because they want to make sure that customers can rely on a consistent level of service. Existing members of staff are expected to sign up for additional shifts to handle increased demand. After completing their first few weeks in a Zappos call center, employees who feel that they haven't developed a strong connection with the company's culture and goals are offered $3,000 to leave. Zappos would rather see people who don't feel aligned with the culture walk away than stay and be unhappy.

To ensure that employees *do* feel comfortable with the culture, managers are expected to spend 10 to 20 percent of their time on team-building activities such as volunteering or even Easter egg hunts. The company holds regular cookouts, family events, parties, and trips to events such as the theater.

Zappos invites employees to forge close relationships with colleagues, giving managers responsibility for assisting employees in developing a career path and creating a culture book that details how people feel about the Zappos culture. When an employee graduates from a training course, the entire department is devoted to celebrating their achievement.

To convince people to buy shoes online, Zappos understands that customers need to feel very good about the level of service they receive, and that requires a tight-knit, happy culture that employees feel proud to be a part of.

SOUTHWEST AIRLINES REPRESENTS HUMOR AND PLAYFULNESS IN FLYING

Southwest Airlines takes a different approach, using humor to show customers that they are respected and appreciated. Known for making flying fun, the company cements that reputation by supporting staff in coming up with ways to enliven the flying experience. It is part of their brand.

Sometimes Southwest pilots emerge from the cockpit to greet passengers as they step on to the plane. Sometimes flight attendants tell jokes while they're making announcements. Interestingly, opening up the potential for unscripted jokes occasionally leads to flight attendants telling jokes that aren't particularly amusing, but Southwest encourages that kind of experimentation because the company feels that even a bad joke, in an effort to entertain passengers, is preferable to a humorless experience.

Telling a joke to an airplane full of passengers is a vulnerable experience, but because the company nurtures an environment in which that experience is normalized, it builds a lot of trust among staff members, and a lot of positivity towards Southwest as a company. Humor occurs between people who trust one another. By leading with humor, Southwest makes the company seem trustable.

CROSSFIT IS TEAM FITNESS

A fourth example is CrossFit, a brand that has mushroomed in popularity over the last few years, and which thrives on creating a group atmosphere in which CrossFit clients can share their vulnerabilities.

When they aren't strong enough to lift a particular weight, or fit enough to complete a tough exercise, CrossFit participants have the opportunity to share their experience and engage the support of their peers. As a result, they quickly feel part of a community, united by shared goals and carried forward by the energy of the group.

Warby Parker, Zappos, Southwest Airlines, and CrossFit all project desirable human qualities: Warby Parker's individuality and quirkiness, Zappos' togetherness, Southwest's humor and playfulness, and CrossFit's mutual support. All depend upon those expressions being respected to sustain their brand, and their customers and clients come to rely on those experiences whenever they interact with those brands. By embodying qualities that people want to experience, they present a very human face and become highly relatable.

Just as brands can express human qualities and elicit emotions, so humans can determine the qualities they want to be recognized for and craft brands based upon their unique strengths. Some people love to make others smile. Others are very adept technically, or are brilliant artists.

A friend of mine trades on the tagline "accelerating serendipity" and excels at connecting people. He has built an entire brand around that skill set, orienting everything from his LinkedIn profile to his e-mail signature around it, and consistently building a network of people he can serve through making valuable connections for them.

Now consider, for a moment, what happens when these brands break their promises. What happens if you walk into a Hilton hotel and they simply tell you that they have no vacancies? What happens if you fly Southwest and the tone of the announcements is dour and humorless? What happens if the man whose brand says that he accelerates serendipity has no interest in meeting new people?

To maintain their integrity, brands need to keep the promises they are making, both to their employees and to their customers. If a brand stakes out a position, and then fails to behave in a manner consistent with that position, that brand's followers will be disappointed.

A brand that betrays the expectations of followers demonstrates disrespect, leading to a loss of trust and loyalty. This applies equally to employees, who may value the opportunity to work with a brand whose principles they appreciate, and customers, who turn to a brand expecting the experience it portrays, and will be disillusioned if it fails to meet those expectations.

This is not to say that a brand can never make mistakes or evolve. The Facebook example earlier in this chapter illustrates the extent to which mistakes can become learning opportunities. Abercrombie & Fitch provides a case study of a company that realized its core demographic was growing older and launched Hollister to appeal to a younger audience.

Whatever transformations a brand undergoes, however, one thing must remain consistent: a commitment to respect the emotions it inspires in its customers and in its employees.

CHAPTER FOUR

LOYALTY BRINGS CONSISTENCY

If the rate of change on the outside exceeds the rate of change on the inside, then the end is near.
—JACK WELCH, FORMER CEO, GENERAL ELECTRIC

What makes a company last?

Most of the business leaders I meet invite me to the table because they want to talk about how technology can help their businesses grow. Yet, I've come to realize that their key concerns aren't about how to achieve short-term growth, but how to achieve sustainable or lasting growth. The secret I've learned is that sustainable growth comes from customers and employees who value the company enough to stay with it and make the adaptations that are necessary to stay relevant over time.

A brief look at history suggests that few companies sustain themselves over decades. This makes it even more valuable to observe the working practices of those that *do* thrive in the long term. A lot can be learned from those companies with years of growth behind them, and those that have taken steps to help them sustain growth in this era of rapid technological change.

Take a look at the current Fortune 500, and guess how many of the companies that were on the list in 1955, the year it was founded, are still there today.

Fifty percent? Seventy percent? Far, far fewer. Only 12.2 percent of the companies listed on the Fortune 500 in 1955 retain their places today.[8] That's sixty-one companies. The other 439, almost 88 percent, have dropped off the list. Half a century ago,[9] the life expectancy of a company on the Fortune 500 was seventy-five years. Today, it is fifteen years, and continues to decline. Of the five thousand publicly traded companies in the United States, only 486 are more than a hundred years old.

Contrast this state of affairs with the situation in Japan. According to the credit rating agency, Tokyo Shoko

Research, there are more than twenty thousand Japanese companies more than a hundred years old, including a few that are more than a thousand years old. The list includes Nissiyama Onsen Keiunkan, a hotel founded in the year 705, which is believed to be the oldest company in the world. The Japanese even have a specific term, *shinise*, for long-lived companies. What, then, is the key to their longevity? Professor Makoto Kanda, who has studied these companies extensively, says that Japanese companies can survive for so long because many are small and family-run, and because they focus on central ethical values that are not exclusively profit based.

That's not to say that Japan offers all the answers to the puzzle of sustainable growth. Many Japanese companies survive for a very long time without ever really growing beyond their local markets. By the same token, the oldest Japanese companies are not the largest. So, what do companies with outstanding longevity, large or small, have in common? They find ways of generating both customer and employee loyalty.

I've identified four primary factors that establish loyalty: **purpose**, **product**, **profit**, and **people**. Let's explore more how different companies demonstrate these factors.

PURPOSE AND MISSION-DRIVEN COMPANIES

Companies that stand for something more profound than simple financial gain have a reason to continue existing during difficult times. This makes them more likely to weather storms and return to prosperity during better days.

Merck is a 120-year-old pharmaceutical company with a stated goal of improving human life. The company was listed on the Fortune 500 in 1955, and although it hasn't been there *every* year since then, it is in 2017. Merck measures corporate success using the yardstick of the company's ability to defeat disease.

IBM is another rare centenarian in an economy populated mainly by teenagers. Founded in the United States in 1911 (the German version of the company is even older), IBM has been driven since its foundation by a simple mission: to help other companies, and individuals, improve their operations. The tools IBM has used to achieve those ends have naturally evolved over the years, from typewriters, to mainframe computers, to personal computing, and now to cloud computing, but the underlying aim has remained constant.

PRODUCT INNOVATION

As the quote that heads this chapter suggests, changing

with the times is an essential aspect of longevity. Companies that thrive in the long-term generally invest heavily in innovation and, where necessary, reinvention.

At 3M, founded in 1902 and with a consistent presence on the Fortune 500 list since 1955, employees are required to spend 15 percent of their time working on side projects. Some of these projects will develop into major business ideas. Others will remain hobbies and curiosities. The important thing from the company's perspective is that employees have the time and space to follow interests and hunches, even if it's not immediately clear where they will lead.

DuPont is even older. The company was founded in 1802 and, again, has featured consistently on the list of Fortune 500 companies since 1955. In 2010, DuPont implemented a new policy insisting that 30 percent of total revenue should come from products developed in the previous four years. The company's leaders determined that sitting on their laurels and continuing to rely on products based on patents that might be decades old would lead them to stagnation and gradual decline, and took action to reverse that trend.

Google was only founded in 1998, but the company illustrates many of the principles that distinguish firms that have been successful for many years. The tech giant may be relatively youthful, but it's astonishingly successful and quick to adopt good ideas. The company operates a similar policy to 3M, encouraging employees to spend 20 percent of their working week on projects outside of their day-to-day responsibility.

In 2006, the companies reporting the greatest spending on research and development were mostly automotive and pharmaceutical firms. In 2016, they were primarily tech companies.[10] The only organization to maintain a steady place in the top five over the past decade is Microsoft. According to PwC, most of the world's major innovators are on the same journey.[11] They are moving into a world where the focus of research and development is shifting towards software and services. New software improves the performance of their products, and services provide customers with additional features and improved usability.

At Microsoft, we regularly assess what percentage of our revenue is coming from more traditional offerings, and how much is flowing from newer, cloud-based services. We want to know, and show, how we're transforming our revenue base through branching out into fresh, modern innovations like cloud computing. When Facebook went public in 2012, the company's number one business challenge was to improve the percentage of advertising revenue generated via mobile. Quarter by quarter, the company is gradually upping that percentage. By January 2016, mobile ads generated 80 percent of Facebook's ad revenue.

The companies that last grow and change, at least as fast as the market grows and changes, and sometimes even faster.

PROFITABILITY, SHORT-TERM AND LONG-TERM

It may seem obvious that profit contributes to longevity. How can a business survive if it isn't making money? What may not be quite so obvious is that it isn't usually a focus on short-term profit that reaps rewards. Instead, companies that focus on strong financial foundations, earning steady revenues from the products or services they sell, attain stability over the long term.

Microsoft was only founded in April 1975, but the company's approach is nonetheless instructive. Having earned significant profits through the success of franchises like Windows, Microsoft gained the financial stability to invest in other product lines, such as Xbox, Bing, and now cloud computing and large data centers around the world. Importantly, it wasn't necessary for those new product lines to become instantly profitable. It was enough for our core business to sustain the company while we explored new avenues.

IBM takes a similar approach, carrying a very low debt burden and investing heavily in innovations that ultimately bring increasing returns to shareholders. Companies that already have a strong balance sheet don't need to solicit outside investment. They are self-sustaining, which allows them to invest surpluses into researching and developing new products and services, without the pressure to show an instant return that would accompany venture capital.

PEOPLE DESERVE INVESTMENT

It may sound like a cliché to say that people are the most important resource any business possesses, but there's research suggesting that it may be true. In *Why Loyalty Matters: The Groundbreaking Approach to Rediscovering Happiness, Meaning and Lasting Fulfillment in Your Life and Work*, Timothy Keiningham and Lerzan Aksoy discuss research comparing the returns from investment in capital improvements, such as new buildings and modern machinery, and the returns gleaned from developing employee capital. For businesses wishing to grow sustainably, the results are very instructive.

On average, investing 10 percent of a company's revenue

in capital improvements yielded a 3.9 percent growth in overall productivity. This gain was sustained year-on-year. Investing 10 percent of a company's revenue in employees, however, produced an average productivity gain of 8.5 percent, or more than twice as much, once again sustained year-on-year.

In a world of choice, where both customers and employees come and go, companies that grow their way out of bad times and excel during good times need customers who will stay with them and employees who are sufficiently loyal and committed to continually increase their productivity.

Successful businesses are built on the good work of employees. Creating and developing a business, be it large or small, demands significant effort. Employees also learn a great deal from doing their jobs over a period of time. If they move on, most of that learning is lost. If they stay within the company, even if they shift roles, the learning is retained and they can transmit it to other employees.

The most sustainable option for an organization is to develop the people who work there so well that they become a resource from which the next generation of leaders and managers can be drawn. Leadership guru Ram Charan suggests that the ultimate goal of management in any organization is to promote the next CEO from within. As an illustration of how valuable this approach can be, consider that forty-seven of the top fifty companies listed on the Fortune 500 found their most recent CEOs internally.

CONSISTENCY THROUGH CHANGE

Change can sweep away companies that once existed, but it can also hold those that survive to a higher standard and usher in innovations that wouldn't otherwise have existed.

If today's Standard and Poor 500 was made up only of the companies that were on the index in 1957, the index's overall performance would be 20 percent poorer than it actually is.[12]

Allowing companies that have run their course to shut down or reinvent themselves can be a positive development, reshaping the economy and increasing productivity. The most productive companies will continue to last, grow and, crucially, to change over the course of many years. Those that have already lasted more than a hundred years have demonstrated an ability to evolve their attitudes and operations in tune with the times. If they are to continue to thrive, they will need to sustain this ability in years to come.

Japanese companies generally don't change, merge, and die at the same rate as American companies, but they also don't grow at the same rate. They generally remain smaller, both in size and scope, than their American counterparts. The challenge many companies face is balancing their ability to grow with their sustainability. The usual pattern is for companies to either lose touch with customers as they grow, and therefore endanger loyalty, or to remain limited in size because they are unable to scale the values that make them successful.

That's the reason why Sam Walton advised small businesses not to compete with Walmart on price, but instead to focus on providing a level of service Walmart can't match.

Companies that succeed, over a long time frame, both in growing and in retaining their best employees and repeat customers, are the ones who crack this conundrum. They are companies that manage to scale loyalty. To do that, they need to be consistently self-sustaining. That requires all four of the factors mentioned earlier to be functioning effectively.

IBM's general purpose is to help other companies improve their operations. To do that, they need products that meet the needs of their clients. In order to *develop* those products without relying on external investment, the company must be financially self-sustaining, with a sufficiently healthy balance sheet to fund research and development into new products.

Finally, to repeatedly create high-quality products, the company needs to attract and keep intelligent, loyal employees, which requires listening to them with curiosity and treating them with respect. If any part of that cycle starts to break down, all the others will be placed under stress and will become increasingly hard to maintain.

In a changing world, self-sustainability is a form of consistency. A company may retain the same name and the same mission, while brands and products evolve. The ability to adapt and move with the times allows the company as an entity to survive, grow, and thrive.

THE LOYALTY HABIT

Are you one of the nearly 250 million people worldwide with an Amazon account? If so, you've probably noticed that every time you visit the Amazon website you receive suggestions based on your interests. When you make a purchase, you're prompted to give feedback on the seller or write a review. Enter your address and payment details, and you can turn on one-click ordering, removing another barrier to purchase.

Amazon has created a highly interactive, digital experience that gives patrons a sense that they are being listened to, and invites them to become habituated to making purchases and providing feedback. The company has done an exceptional job of crafting a digital experience that allows customers to feel that they are listened to and respected. In a high-tech environment, the Amazon website presents a uniquely personalized experience to each user.

As a result, millions of people trust Amazon enough to allow the company to make suggestions about what they buy. When they need a new book, or want to watch a movie, they open up the Amazon website and look at what Amazon recommends. As yet, this is the nearest mainstream digital equivalent of the obliging general store employee who knew the preferences of their customers and was always willing to help them find what they needed.

Buying from Amazon becomes a habit in the way that going to the general store used to be a habit or, in the modern era, visiting the supermarket is a habit. Every click breeds loyalty. Every click reinforces the message that Amazon is a good place to buy online.

That is not a coincidence. Amazon goes to a lot of effort to acquire customers and take care of them, because the company knows that a loyal customer who makes Amazon their first choice whenever they need to make an online purchase is enormously valuable in terms of lifetime value. They develop a relationship with the brand and trust Amazon to solve their problems.

Of course, habits can be broken. Loyalty can fade. If Amazon ceased to provide those services and responded poorly or slowly to customer feedback, it could soon lose the loyalty it has accrued, and people would forge new habits elsewhere. The company rarely engages with customers over the phone, and it largely doesn't operate retail locations, so the way Amazon team members address customer concerns is via e-mail, which is of paramount importance, as is the accuracy and relevance of recommendations.

No organization, of course, is completely flawless. A positive feeling towards a company accumulates steadily when that company provides clientele with an experience they appreciate. After a while, the reserve of goodwill grows to a point that companies can afford to mess up occasionally and still retain loyalty, as long as they handle their mistakes with transparency and learn from them. A company that fails to maintain those standards, however, and begins to give customers fewer positive experiences and more negative ones, will gradually find its customer base shrinking.

In order to create positive experiences for customers and clients, companies must also be in the business of creating positive experiences for employees. Apple is a good example of this phenomenon. Employees at Apple stores are encouraged to spend time with customers to understand their needs and give them an experience of being listened to.

When the time comes to make a purchase, many customers allow Apple employees to make the right recommendation for them, and walk out thanking the associate for their time and input. That's a very high level of trust, and it's only possible because employees are respected for their contributions and expected to take the time necessary to build relationships with customers. That leads to a high level of loyalty among Apple employees, and to the retention of skills as they remain with the company, keep learning, and teach newer employees what they already know.

Another aspect of Apple stores is that there's no VIP shortcut. Customers take a ticket and wait in line until their turn comes. This contributes to an atmosphere of fairness and a sense that every customer, however new or old, is valued equally. Employees build solid relationships with peers and managers, and that trust invites the possibility of innovation. Failure is tolerated as long as it is turned into a learning opportunity. That experience is hard to replicate for any employee thinking of leaving the company, making it much more likely that they'll stay.

On the other hand, companies that have very high employee turnover never instill this level of loyalty. They tend to rely on rigid protocols, because they can't or don't trust their employees to think and act for themselves. This creates a vicious circle, where those employees leave as soon as possible because their working experience is limiting and deadening. As a result, managers and employees never develop a trusting relationship, and there are few effective ambassadors of the company's culture and values.

Employees don't feel comfortable speaking up to suggest improvements to products and processes, impoverishing the company's intellectual capital, and the company finds itself in a downward spiral, hemorrhaging the resources needed to be successful. This has a corrosive effect. According to *Harvard Business Review*, which investigated companies where employees were afraid to speak up, and explored the reasons why:

"[Many] were inhibited by broad, often vague, perceptions about the work environment. Many people reported withholding input from a person higher up in the corporate hierarchy because they believed (without any evidence) that the superior felt ownership of the project, process, or issue in question and would resent suggestions that implied a need for change.

Employees also believed (again without direct experience) that their bosses would feel betrayed if constructive ideas for change were offered when more senior leaders were present or that their bosses would feel embarrassed to be shown up by a subordinate in front of other subordinates.[13]"

Contrast that with the approach taken by Starbucks. The company has built an integrated system for training and supporting employees. As such a large employer, training so many people, Starbucks is now one of the largest educational institutions in the United States. New employees can expect that, when they arrive in a new store, they will be greeted by managers and employees who have been there for some time and who will make them feel comfortable. They're encouraged to share customer feedback and ideas of how the company can improve its processes, while simultaneously absorbing the company's culture and understanding what it stands for.

Starbucks teaches employees that the company has their back. Their training material details a story about an employee of Starbucks who, as a young man, was never particularly confident. After he was employed by the company, he rose to become a manager. He began to teach employees to see their apron as a shield and remember that they are always protected, no matter what rude and unpleasant customers say.

Starbucks teaches employees how to respond to specific behavioral triggers, and identify the concerns of rude customers. Is the customer upset because they don't like the product, for example, or because they're in a hurry and they feel that the wait is too long?

By investing so much in education and training, Starbucks gives employees the confidence to feel that their contributions are respected, and to recognize that when a customer is rude to them, it's not their fault. Because of this, employees feel protected and confident in representing the brand.

In the auto industry, Tesla has taken this principle even further. In February 2016, a venture capitalist in California wrote a blog post criticizing the way Tesla does business. The company responded by dropping his order. Tesla's CEO, Elon Musk, tweeted that the man was "denied service for being a super rude customer."

For many companies, this attitude seems revolutionary. For Tesla, however, it makes total sense. The company values the morale of employees, and trusts the quality of its products enough to recognize that losing one customer will not harm the bottom line. At the same time, by exercising the privilege to choose whom the company does business with, Tesla is strengthening the values of the brand and sending a clear message that rudeness will not be tolerated.

The principle behind Tesla's decision is that taking on a customer whose behavior impacts negatively on employees is such a drain on the brand's resources that it's simply not worth the time and effort required to do successfully. How would you feel, as an employee, if your CEO stated flatly that customers who made your life difficult and spoke negatively of you and your colleagues were simply not valuable enough to the company to retain them? Probably, you'd be proud that your company appreciated your work and respected your contribution enough to prevent it from being defamed without consequence, leading to an increase in your sense of belonging and loyalty.

Stew Leonard's, a famous grocery store in Connecticut, has two rules etched in granite outside the store: 1) The customer is always right; 2) If the customer is ever wrong, reread rule one.

For that particular company, those principles make sense. The brand's entire identity is based upon providing outstanding service. That's what customers expect and are willing to pay for, and it's what employees know they must provide. Assuming that the customer is right may imply listening to the customer and finding the validity in their perspective, even if it's not immediately obvious. Maybe the dissatisfied customer has an idea that could improve service in the store.

On the other hand, presuming the customer is always right doesn't mean accepting that they have free rein to speak ill of the company, and Tesla illustrates the value of cutting a customer loose when they prove to be more trouble than they're worth.

In 2016, the state of North Carolina passed a law preventing transgender people from using public bathrooms that match their gender identity. In response, PayPal canceled plans to open a new office in the state, sending a very clear message that the company doesn't want to do business in a state where the values of openness and acceptance are not supported. This was broadly seen as a positive move from the company, because it expressed respect and solidarity for those who would otherwise have been marginalized by the law in question.

Google chose not to do business in China because the company didn't feel aligned with the values of the Chinese Government. In the United States, thousands of people boycotted Chick-Fil-A when the company spoke out against homosexuality.

These are examples of customers as investors, in the sense that Google was a potential investor in the Chinese Government and PayPal was a potential investor in the state of North Carolina, choosing not to give their business to institutions they didn't feel aligned with. Each one showcases a different approach, and yet they all illustrate different facets of loyalty.

Amazon generates loyalty by offering customers a personalized online experience. Apple does the same by providing a high level of interaction and support in-store. For Starbucks, loyalty means protecting their employees from rude and unpleasant customers. For Tesla, it is the right to deny service to a customer who attacks the company. For Stew Leonard's, meanwhile, loyalty is the promise of outstanding customer service.

Google is loyal to a belief in transparency and openness that prohibits the company from doing business with those it doesn't believe supports those values, and PayPal expresses loyalty to the characteristics of acceptance and compassion by declining the opportunity to expand their business in North Carolina.

However much their styles vary, all these business are adopting strategies that breed customer loyalty. Customer loyalty is incredibly valuable to businesses with the ambition to grow, because loyal customers recruit other customers.

Word of mouth is the oldest and still the most effective form of marketing. When our friends tell us that something is good, we believe them. Not only do loyal customers continue to make purchases, they spread the word.

What is so notable about the different approaches discussed above is that they appeal to different demographics. While Stew Leonard's sends the message that the customer is always right, Elon Musk is perfectly willing to come out and say that a particular customer is wrong. Yet, both instill loyalty. Stew Leonard's attracts people who value giving and receiving the best possible service. Tesla generates loyalty by standing up for the right of the company to refuse service entirely to customers who make employees' lives difficult.

The stands the two businesses take may appear diametrically opposed, but the results are remarkably similar.

CUSTOMER SATISFACTION VERSUS CUSTOMER LOYALTY

A lot of businesses measure their success in terms of customer satisfaction. While it's undoubtedly a good idea to satisfy customers, that doesn't mean they'll come back when they're next in the market for a product or service. Loyal customers will return again and again, and they'll probably bring their friends.

Every business has a narrative that drives the behavior of employees and, by association, customers. They create those narratives through the experiences they provide. PayPal, by electing not to open an office in North Carolina, forged a narrative in which the company only does business in places where all people are respected. The manager at Starbucks who taught staff to perceive their aprons as shields instituted a narrative that Starbucks was a safe place to work.

Customers and potential customers, employees, and potential employees, gather narratives and use them to determine which companies they want to interact with, and how.

In *Customer Satisfaction is Worthless, Customer Loyalty is Priceless*, Jeffrey Gitomer relates a very interesting story of a hotel guest. The guest arrived at the hotel and was disappointed to discover that there was no ironing board available. The guest needed to iron a shirt for a function. When he asked at the front desk, he was told that no ironing board was available and, when he pressed for a better resolution, the receptionist simply told him there was a store nearby where he could purchase an ironing board.

Now imagine if the receptionist had taken the initiative to procure an ironing board and bring it back for the guest. The guest's mood would probably have shifted immediately from dissatisfaction to elation. He would have had a memorable experience of amazing service, which he would likely have shared extensively. Instead, because that gesture wasn't part of the hotel's narrative about how guests were treated, and it wasn't part of the receptionist's mindset, the guest shared with others a story detailing his disenchantment.

Creating the conditions in which that experience could have occurred is a matter of asking different questions.

A hotel that asks guests whether they enjoyed their stay will receive very different feedback from one in which guests are asked, "Did any of our employees create a memorable experience that you'd like to share with us?" The former inquiry will reveal broadly positive experiences and uncover obvious complaints. The latter will encourage guests to share moments that have made their stay special, and employees to provide those experiences.

A hotel that asks the question, "Did any of our employees create a memorable experience that you'd like to share with us?" is a hotel where memorable experiences are created.

Consumption-based companies, such as mobile phone providers, rely heavily on customer loyalty. Their profit comes from the repeated usage of their services, so their businesses are only successful if customers are happy and satisfied enough to keep using their products, and preferably use them more and more.

Salesforce.com employs "customer success managers," whose specific role is to help customers get more value out of their products. Their responsibility is to talk to new customers and find out how those customers could be getting greater value from the products they've purchased. It's a service they provide, because they understand that customers who value using their products will continue to be customers. They will make more purchases, use more advanced features, and feel happier with their experience of the company.

Once again, the difference is the company's capacity to

listen. The customer success manager has a mandate to listen, to understand each customer's questions, concerns, and interests, and to serve them in resolving their difficulties and meeting their needs. If they do that successfully, they will engender loyalty.

Another area in which loyalty is integral to success is the restaurant business. If you visit a restaurant, and you feel that the waiter or waitress forms a personal connection with you and cares about the quality of your meal and your overall experience, you're more likely both to tip them well and to return.

Think for a moment about your favorite restaurant, and what makes you want to go back. Probably there's something about the ethos that you appreciate. Perhaps the restaurant serves organic or local food, or serves a style of cuisine you particularly enjoy. Perhaps the food is healthy, or the prices are especially good. In all likelihood, you're also enticed by the décor and the atmosphere of the restaurant. It feels good to be there.

Now imagine that the next time you go there, the members of staff pay little attention to you. They seem uninterested in your order or your appetite. They don't smile when they bring your food. They don't inquire whether you enjoyed your meal. Would you go back?

The experience of being consistently listened to is essential to the development of loyalty. Feeling that people care about and respect you, and that they understand your needs and help you fulfill those needs, is vital. Without that feeling, your favorite restaurant becomes just another place to eat.

Danny Meyer, a chef and restaurateur who owns several restaurants in New York, has been experimenting with increasing the wages and benefits of employees, instead of making them reliant on tips. The theory behind this move is that it will create a better experience for everyone, because staff will be comfortable that their basic needs will be met, and that important costs such as healthcare insurance will be covered.

As a result, they will be happier and more attentive to customers. Simultaneously, diners will be freed of any anxiety they might feel about how much to tip, and therefore more relaxed. At the time of writing, it remains to be seen whether Danny Meyer's experiment will prove successful. What is clear, however, is that it aligns closely with many of the principles described in this book.

By specializing in the restaurant business, Danny Meyer has narrowed his focus enough to consider specific improvements to the way he does business. Through listening with curiosity, he has uncovered a problem with which many people who work in service industries are faced.

By respecting their needs, he has hit upon an innovation with the potential to transform their experience. Should the experiment succeed, Danny Meyer can expect strong staff retention rates, with a corresponding increase in collective knowledge and experience.

The consistent presence of happy, skilled employees is a recipe for outstanding dining experiences. Outstanding dining experiences lead to loyal customers, who return again and again to eat at their favorite restaurant.

CONSISTENCY IN A CHANGING WORLD

The business world is changing rapidly. While many companies are being swallowed up by the shifts, others are flourishing. Japanese companies demonstrate the value of consistency, in some cases over the course of hundreds of years, but don't readily present a model for generating loyalty on a large scale.

Sustaining growth in uncertain times necessitates a sense of consistency, which can only come from the loyalty of both employees and customers. Companies that understand how to generate loyalty have a huge advantage over those that do not. As the diverse examples in this chapter illustrate, there is no single path towards loyalty, but there are common characteristics.

People respond to narratives they can relate to, and become loyal to companies that continuously deliver on those narratives. Brands that lose touch with the values they represent, and the ways in which those values are presented to employees and customers, stumble in creating loyalty.

Those that are consistent in exercising their values, meanwhile, and whose business activities and financial foundations are in alignment with those values, act like magnets to skilled employees and loyal customers. These are the companies that have the greatest chance of surviving and thriving in a changing world.

TECHNIQUES FOR DEVELOPING EMPLOYEE LOYALTY

Companies that want to develop customer loyalty need to aspire to retain long-serving employees, who will maintain the culture and teach younger generations. One of the keys to doing this is to provide variety within the context of a single company.

At Microsoft, we have traditionally operated a culture

where people typically stay in a role for two to three years, and can do many different jobs over the course of a career with the company. This cycle is a legacy of the period during which most of Microsoft's employees were engineers, and product cycles were approximately two to three years. Engineers would complete one project and move on to another.

The principle has many benefits, because smart, motivated people like to be constantly learning, so giving them an opportunity to switch roles helps to keep them engaged. A downside of that approach was that the company had very little institutional memory. Engineers may have been at Microsoft for some years, but no one around them was working with a particular team or a specific product for very long, making it harder to remember what had worked or not worked previously. Another was that we imported that culture from our engineering business and transplanted it to our sales and marketing departments, where longer-term, personal relationships are critical to building trust.

Similarly, account managers get to know clients' businesses very well, and when they move on, it can create disruption. As a company, we've altered our overall approach so that where it makes sense, people can shift roles with almost no minimum time in a particular role.

This works well for certain short-term, start-up projects. Employees in customer-facing positions, however, or more senior positions, such as country management, are expected to make a longer-term commitment.

As a manager, I always seek to instill some level of consistency into a team culture, even when working on a short-term project. A few years ago, I took over a team that had experienced a lot of change. Several people had left, and I found there were others who weren't occupying the roles best suited to their skills, so it was necessary to make even more changes.

It was a disruptive experience. Later, when the department settled down, it was important to bring some consistency to the team's working experience. The objective was to retain existing employees, so we could begin to rebuild as a team and return to growth. My managers and I initiated monthly calls, which everyone was expected to attend, and in which the format was very specific. In addition, I encouraged managers to create their own processes for running weekly departmental meetings. The goal of this approach was to bring some stability to the team, so that some elements of the job felt predictable. Eventually, this helped to create a culture of consistency.

Long-term employees are a source of valuable experience and information that cannot be easily replicated by new employees. They understand how and why things happen, and they have the potential to share what they've learned through years of successes and failures. They've already made mistakes, so new employees don't have to do the same.

Typically, this leads to an improved bottom line. New people need to be trained. They need mentors they can turn to for support. A company in which new employees outnumber more seasoned ones can be unstable, with too many people in need of support and too few able to provide it. Hiring new people and letting others go is also very costly. Separation fees, exit interviews, administration, advertising, screening applicants, and conducting interviews all take time and drain resources. A study conducted by the Center for American Progress in 2012[14] concluded that the average cost of replacing a departed employee is approximately one-fifth of their annual salary.

The presence of long-term employees is a good sign when assessing the quality of a company and how pleasant it is to work there. Japanese companies, with their relatively high levels of longevity, often seek employees that want to stay with the company for a long time. In the United States, the opposite is true. In 1980, 51 percent of men aged between thirty-five and sixty-two had been in their jobs more than ten years. By 2005, that number was down to 39 percent. Currently, the average American worker has been in their job only 4.4 years.[15]

As we've seen during this chapter, no company, or country, has all the answers. The Japanese model promotes longevity and stability, but it can limit innovation and scale. The American approach, by contrast, facilitates rapid change but can be disorientating and make it harder to achieve long-term consistency. As the Buddhists understand, the only constant is change, but human beings require a sense of calm and constancy in order to function optimally. The effective organization, which values loyalty and respects employees, will find ways of instilling consistency in the midst of change.

CHAPTER FIVE

LISTENING FUELS INNOVATION

> *@elonmusk The San Mateo supercharger is always full with idiots who leave their Tesla for hours even if already charged.*
> —LOIC LE MEUR, VIA TWITTER

> *@loic You're right, this is becoming an issue. Supercharger spots are meant for charging, not parking. Will take action.*
> —ELON MUSK, CEO OF TESLA, IN RESPONSE

Whenever I meet the founder of a business, I ask them what led them to create their company. Mostly, the answers I hear are similar to the ones you may have heard if you watch the popular television show *Shark Tank*.

In the majority of cases, the founder solved a problem or developed a better way to do something. Described another way, these entrepreneurs listened to others, and sometimes to themselves, to truly understand the root cause of some frustration. Then, they found a way to provide better, cheaper, or easier solutions.

Big companies go through the same process. The way they find solutions may differ in each case, but it always starts with good listening. In the example that opens this chapter, Tesla took a mere six days to craft the following policy and make an announcement on the company's official website[16]:

> "We designed the Supercharger network to enable a seamless, enjoyable road trip experience. Therefore, we understand that it can be frustrating to arrive at a station only to discover fully-charged Tesla cars occupying all the spots. To create a better experience for all owners, we're introducing a fleet-wide idle fee that aims to increase Supercharger availability."

Many businesses tell stories that hinge on the moment when their founders listened carefully to the needs of customers and potential customers, and tailored their offerings to meet those needs. H. J. Heinz, the founder of the most famous tomato ketchup company in the world, started his business journey when he was just eight years old, selling spare produce from his mother's vegetable garden to neighbors.

This initial bloom of entrepreneurship soon blossomed into a thriving pickle, sauerkraut, and vinegar business and, eventually, the iconic Heinz tomato ketchup. Heinz's true innovation, however, was to listen to customers who told him that green and brown sauce bottles left them feeling uncertain of what they were buying, and unsure whether they could trust the quality of the product.

The clear glass in which he packed his tomato ketchup allowed customers to see the quality and purity of his product. This is a motif that the company revisited years later, running a famous commercial highlighting how slowly it emerged from the bottle. The message was that the thick consistency of Heinz ketchup was a reliable indication of quality. H. J. Heinz built what has become a global brand on an ability to listen to customers, understand their concerns, and respond accordingly.

More recently, the founders of Uber tapped into the frustration they and their friends felt traveling around cities. They didn't want to own a car, but they needed regular, cost-effective access to transportation. They came up with a solution that connected owner-drivers with people who needed transportation, and Uber was born.

Innovation happens when people take the time to understand a problem, and have the creativity to develop an original solution. Kickstarter, as discussed in chapter three, is a platform based upon listening. People who set up a Kickstarter campaign are betting that they have successfully solved a problem that others deem important, and their campaign is the laboratory in which they get the opportunity to find out whether they're correct. They receive feedback in the form of discovering whether people like their idea enough to support it financially. If they're open to them, they may receive ideas about how they can make their product better.

Right from the inception of their company, before they've even created their products, they have the opportunity to listen to what people think of their ideas. This can save them a lot of money, which they would otherwise have had to spend in order to produce and test prototypes.

Open sourcing, by inviting all the members of a community to contribute their feedback and ideas during the development of a product, is another method of listening. Authors often do this with chapters of their books. On a far larger scale, the Shenzhen ecosystem in China is a large-scale manufacturer of electronics and electronic components, especially mobile phones and computers.

Shenzhen is essentially an entire city based on immediate customer feedback, which is used to drive new product innovation. It's possible to manufacture a new model of mobile phone in the city, stand outside on the street and sell it to passersby, and use feedback received from those customers to produce a modified version the following day.

The production cycle in Shenzhen has become so short that it's possible to solicit customer feedback almost immediately, and for products to evolve incredibly rapidly.

Xiaomi, a Chinese mobile phone company based in Shenzhen, found initial success by listening closely to what people were buying and monitoring hardware trends in real time. By doing so, they were able to alter their own products at extraordinary speeds. New companies, such as Oppo and Vivo, have quickly recreated their model, also with considerable success.

In the United States, Samsung has arguably remained competitive with Apple primarily by responding so swiftly to feedback received from users, and by shipping new products at an equally accelerated rate. Despite being perceived as a top-down enterprise, Apple is another exceptionally responsive company. By evaluating feedback received from online chat services and discussion boards, from reviews, and even from calls made to customer support, the company is able to quickly assess where small tweaks or updates would be beneficial.

From the low-tech listening methods of H. J. Heinz, walking the streets of the towns where he sold his sauces and listening to his customers, to the very high-tech data gathering practiced by Samsung and Apple, collecting relevant information has always been essential to driving innovation.

People purchase products that solve their problems, or provide them with emotions they wish to feel. The more effectively a company can listen to their customers, the more capably it can meet those needs.

THE SPICE RACK CYCLE: ALWAYS BE CREATING DISRUPTIVE INNOVATION

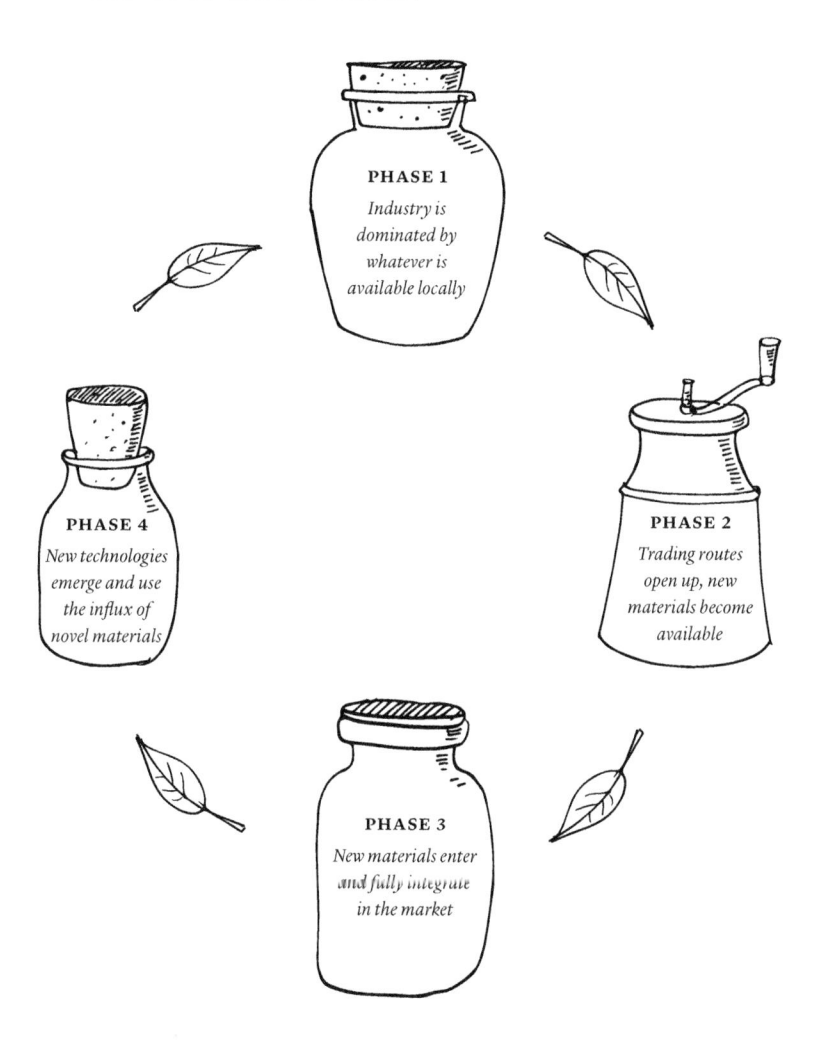

PHASE 1
Industry is dominated by whatever is available locally

PHASE 2
Trading routes open up, new materials become available

PHASE 3
New materials enter and fully integrate in the market

PHASE 4
New technologies emerge and use the influx of novel materials

Before the spice rack became a fixture in Western kitchens, most people relied on herbs and condiments that were grown or gathered locally. The advent of long-distance trade allowed people to sample exotic new flavors and aromas, preserved and bottled to maintain their freshness.

Eventually, imported spices became so commonplace that those amenable to local climates began to be grown in the regions they had been imported to. With care, gardeners were sometimes able to cultivate improved versions of the original spices: a chili with a greater kick, or a delicate strain of saffron.

As technological advances have kicked in, growing conditions have changed. Polytunnels and hydroponics are now regular fixtures in urban market gardens, and bring greater yields, high quality, and the capacity to regulate growing conditions, allowing crops that might otherwise be hard to cultivate successfully to be grown in seemingly unfavorable conditions.

These are the four phases of the Spice Rack Cycle. In the initial phase, an industry is dominated by whatever is available locally. People grow, make, or trade whatever they can access from within the region where they live.

In the second phase, trading routes open up and new materials become available. These new materials disrupt and transform the industry, shifting the parameters of what can be achieved and introducing people to new experiences.

By the third phase, the new materials that have entered the market are fully integrated into the original market. In the case of spices, this happened when imported spices began to make their way into local dishes, and cuisines, and culinary tastes evolved as a result.

Finally, in the fourth phase of the Spice Rack Cycle, new technologies spring up to take advantage of the influx of novel materials. Hydroponics and polytunnels are examples of this, allowing once exotic spices to be grown in new, unfamiliar climatic conditions.

In London, there's a highly innovative project named Growing Underground, in which crops are being grown in old, abandoned bomb shelters and military bunkers. Growing Underground started by populating an old World War II bomb shelter, and proceeded to transform it into a thirty-three-meter (108-foot) farm, situated below pavement level.

In that space, the company has succeeded in growing delicious fresh microgreens and herbs that are highly nutritious, use 70 percent less water than traditional farms, and have a very low carbon footprint. The whole project is powered by an array of digital sensors that monitor the growth of the plants remotely, delivering water at appropriate intervals.

Nearly every industry goes through some version of the Spice Rack Cycle as it changes, evolves, and absorbs new influences and finding ways to adapt.

In more developed regions, the advent of canned food was a disruption to the traditional practice of growing fresh food locally. That made numerous new flavors and dishes commonplace, but had the drawback that canned food lacks the flavor and nutritional quality of fresh food.

The next step was for farmers and gardeners to set about producing foods that were only available in canned form locally. Now there are further innovations with new strains of crops, and even new types of meat, being developed.

Let's illustrate the process with a familiar example. Traditionally, if you wanted to get from location A to B in a big city you didn't know well, you would probably hail a taxi. The taxi driver, with their encyclopedic knowledge of their local streets, would take you where you wanted to go (you would have to trust them to take the fastest route).

The advent of Uber disrupted that business model. Now,

instead of taking a taxi, you probably use Uber instead. The prices are cheaper, it's more convenient, and as long as all goes as planned, there's no loss of service.

Far from being the endgame, however, Uber is only the beginning of disruptions to the taxi industry. In many countries, local taxi services are creating their own applications, which combine the value and ease of Uber with the feel-good factor of supporting the local economy.

What will the next phase be? I suspect that it will involve improvements on the standard Uber model. For example, perhaps some companies will initiate their own Uber-esque services, where the cars are all of an especially high quality, or the drivers have exemplary safety records, or passengers can access free Wi-Fi while they travel.

This list is by no means exhaustive. Instead, it is intended to demonstrate how many directions an industry can develop in, once it has been disrupted and opened to new possibilities.

In the hospitality industry, Airbnb effectively showcases the potential for disruption. In phase one of the Spice Rack Cycle, people habitually booked hotels or guesthouses when they needed places to stay while visiting another city. Airbnb is phase two, challenging the belief that a hotel is the natural option and opening up a cornucopia of new possibilities to both business and leisure travelers. Instead of relying on hotels, people are surfing Airbnb in search of apartments or rooms in people's houses.

As phase three takes hold, people are wondering how they can guarantee the quality of their accommodations. Hotels are taking advantage of websites such as TripAdvisor, and offering exceptional late deals, to combine the professionalism and reassurance of a hotel with the flexibility and budget-friendly approach of Airbnb.

Phase four, the integration of all those influences, is already beginning to take shape. Some companies are using Airbnb for their business travelers, giving them a unique source of leverage because they may be booking for many people at a time, and also because they will probably become repeat customers if they receive good service.

At some stage, we may see companies such as Hilton or Hyatt managing Airbnb properties, bringing with them the guarantee of quality that is a defining characteristic of their brands.

The Spice Rack Cycle, or some version of it, affects every industry. Businesses that listen to their customers drive the changes, or become aware of them while they are in their early stages. Those are the businesses that have the greatest opportunity to respond effectively and turn the Spice Rack Cycle to their advantage.

Businesses that neglect the importance of listening are the ones that find themselves overtaken by the Spice Rack Cycle, and losing trade. Some recover, others do not.

The key to understanding the Spice Rack Cycle is to recognize that the initial disruption is only part of the process, not its conclusion. If Uber doesn't listen when drivers offer feedback on how it can improve services, it will soon be overtaken by other innovations. If Airbnb doesn't find a way of assuring clients that the quality and location of their accommodations are good, it will suffer in comparison with other companies that do.

The more global a product or service, the more tailoring it to a local audience pays dividends. The reverse is also true. Localized businesses can benefit enormously from integrating their operations with global technologies.

When Microsoft was in its infancy, the company was focused on putting a PC on every desk and in every home, and connecting people around the world with the power of computing. Nowadays, some of the company's most far-reaching developments involve localizing products to utilize a specific language that may be spoken by a relatively small number of people. At the extreme, this can mean making Microsoft products available to villages in Africa, where the indigenous languages are spoken by no more than a few hundred people.

Once a market has been disrupted, it's relatively easy for new innovations to gain traction. The market has already illustrated that it's open to change, so further change is a relatively small step. The process of innovation requires continual listening and a continual feedback loop with customers.

American Express is an example of a company that had a powerful position in the market, and has slipped somewhat because other companies have listened more carefully and innovated more swiftly. The company was a renowned leader in the premium financial services market. They were one of the first companies to issue a high-end credit card, a charge card, and a platinum card, and to prove that people were willing to pay for those services.

At the time, those innovations altered the market significantly. They made American Express very successful, and they created a template that other financial services organizations sought to emulate. The Chase Sapphire Reserve card, for example, premiered in late 2016, and saw significant adoption among customers not traditionally interested in high-end credit or charge cards. The oversubscription was so great that according to CEO Jamie Dimon, the new card reduced JPMorgan Chase & Co.'s profits by $200 million during the fourth quarter of 2016. While this may initially seem like a negative impact, however, the company expects to more than recoup its losses over the lifetime of customers.

While American Express states publicly that business is strong, the company created the market and has seen its position decline over the years. As yet, it hasn't fully answered the challenges posed by competitors. The company remains a big player in the financial services market, but it is not as unique or as well differentiated as it once was.

I recently heard the current CEO of PayPal, who is a former employee of American Express, discuss his reasons for leaving the latter. He said that his role, which involved spearheading new and innovative business models for the company, was difficult to fulfill, because he found that he wasn't able to transform the culture at American Express in ways that he felt were necessary.

Arguably, the company was so committed to its existing business model that it was limited in its capacity to seriously entertain more significant changes or improvements.

This led to it losing market share, and also losing the loyalty of the employee whose responsibility it was to drive innovation within the company.

Kodak is another example of a company that suffered when the industry in which it operated was disrupted. One of the giants of analog photography, Kodak was, ironically, one of the first companies to see the digital wave coming and attempted to adapt. Unfortunately, however, the company's efforts to innovate were not effective. Ultimately, Kodak declined when demand for the services on which they built their business faded.

In 1996, on the back of the Olympics in Atlanta, Kodak launched a new hybrid service, incorporating the enhancements of digital photography into their more traditional analog business. Essentially, Kodak sought to sustain its existing customer base and business model, while simultaneously introducing them to the advantages of digital. The problem was that Kodak didn't go all the way.

To process the new hybrid film, it was still necessary to take it into a processing facility and wait at least twenty-four hours for it to be ready. Photographs, once processed, were received in printed form, much like the old analog images that Kodak previously specialized in.

Kodak saw the digital revolution coming, but didn't realize how profound it was shaping up to be. Later, mobile phones began to sport cameras capable of capturing images in high resolution, and Facebook, Instagram, Twitter, and Tumblr gave people platforms on which to share their creative expressions.

Kodak represented phase one of the Spice Rack Cycle. The digital disruption to their business represented phase two. Arguably, the craze for filters such as the ones provided by Instagram, and for the instantaneous hit provided by Snapchat, represent phase three.

So, what's phase four, and how can companies that have lost their way in the marketplace win back the customers they have lost?

In Kodak's case, what's immediately obvious is that the company still retains a reputation for quality in its core business. The problem is that that core business has been marginalized. In theory, the company could benefit from reassessing its strengths and determining where it still has a lot to offer.

What is its core competency, and where are the people who value that core competency? Does the company still have strong, loyal employees? Does it own patents or intellectual property that remain valuable?

Kodak did once have loyal customers who appreciated the attributes of the company's brand. Perhaps they could trade on that long heritage to provide more specialized services to people who want to capture especially high-quality images with vintage filters. Possibly they could leverage the nostalgia people still feel for the past by developing digital cameras that recreate that grainy, otherworldly feel.

In Kodak's case, it may be too late to change. It's clear that Instagram has a firm grip on the marketplace for people who want to take photos quickly, want them to look good and be easy to manipulate, and want to be able to share them with friends. Nonetheless, the principle remains. Companies that are losing market share need to listen to their remaining customers, request their feedback, and understand their challenges. Only then do they have a chance of regaining their business.

Most of us take the presence of a spice rack in our kitchens for granted nowadays, but there was a time when imported spices were a rare and highly prized delicacy. In the same fashion, many markets are undergoing evolution as they tread a similar path to the one trodden by the condiments industry.

As once-exotic spices became commonplace, integrated into new regional cuisines, were cultivated in their new locales, and now are subject to new technologies such as the pioneering Growing Underground project in London, so other industries are undergoing their versions of the Spice Rack Cycle.

They are at different stages, and their outcomes look slightly different, but all follow similar principles when incorporating new and disruptive influences. In a globalized economy, as the potential for connecting in new ways continues to grow, it's debatable whether any industry is immune to being disrupted. The companies that survive and thrive in times of disruption are the ones that succeed in listening effectively to their customers and using the information they receive to fuel innovation.

MAPPING THE SPICE RACK CYCLE: AUTOMATION, BIG SCALE, COMPUTER-ASSISTED PRODUCTION, DIGITAL CREATION

The four stages of the Spice Rack Cycle invite comparison with the four industrial revolutions.

The first stage correlates with the **automation** that was characteristic of the First Industrial Revolution, driven by manual labor and steam power.

The second bears comparison with the **big-scale growth** that became possible when mass production was combined with electricity.

The third stage of the Spice Rack Cycle has a parallel with **computer-assisted production and global distribution**, enabled by electronics and IT.

Finally, the fourth stage is represented by **digital creation** and by the **ubiquitous consumption** delivered by **cloud computing**. This stage often involves a return to the emotions invoked by the first stage, when local production and distribution were the norm, albeit at a far larger scale.

While every industry passes through these four stages, not all have yet reached stage four. The transportation industry began with steam engines for automation and progressed to the internal combustion engine and the vehicles that incorporated it, at scale.

Uber is an example of using computers to enhance the transport experience. Another example is the development of hybrid cars, fitted with electronic batteries that complement the internal combustion engines. The fourth phase of the Spice Rack Cycle, digital innovation, is only just emerging in the transportation industry. Driverless cars are one possibility, as are partnerships between car manufacturers and services such as Uber and Lyft to create rapid, large-scale, on-demand services.

A similar evolution has taken place in the news industry. As far back as Roman times, couriers delivered transported wax tablets that served as messaging systems and could be wiped clean and reused. In the seventeenth century, the import of coffee led to the formation of coffee houses where people congregated to discuss the issues of the day.

The first recognizably weekly newspaper, however, originated in Europe in 1605 and was known as *Relation* or *The Account of All Distinguished and Commemorable News*. The invention of the printing press took newspapers into a new era, subsequently augmented by mass production and distribution of daily newspapers, the advent of radio, and the invention of television.

The Internet brought news into the third phase of the Spice Rack Cycle, allowing anyone to create a website and share reports, commentary, and opinions on a global scale. Now, in the digital era, we're starting to see customized news and recommended reading based upon machine learning.

Periscope, Twitter, and Facebook Live offer instant live streaming of events and invite commentary, debate, and sharing. Once again, as the production and distribution of news becomes more universal, the *experience* becomes more participatory and local. Just as in the coffee houses of the seventeenth century, we all have the opportunity to get involved in current affairs and contribute to an ongoing discussion. During the US presidential election cycle in 2016, Donald Trump harnessed the power of Twitter to communicate directly with supporters and respond to challengers.

Let's conclude this chapter by taking two more industries through the entire cycle. "Which industries," you ask? Two of the most ubiquitous: the generation of electricity and the humble toilet.

The generation of electricity is, perhaps surprisingly, a story that starts at the local level. Before it became cost-effective enough to merit the creation of a national grid, electricity was largely a luxury for wealthy individuals and neighborhoods. Initially, the distribution was very small scale.

Before long, it became possible to generate electricity

more cheaply and easily, and numerous providers began to compete to supply towns and cities with electricity. This was the disruptive automation phase, with the existing network of locally-generated electricity challenged by the increasing ubiquity of a larger grid.

As the electrical grid penetrated many more households, until it became almost universal in more developed countries, the competition died down and a few larger companies gradually took over. In some countries, governments took over and began to run services as a public utility.

This combined the local element of having an outlet in the region with a bigger scale outlook that took advantage of economies of scale. A larger regional or national grid enabled cheaper electricity supply, and also reduced the risk of outages, because it became possible to divert surpluses from one area of the grid to places where there was a shortage, with the assistance of computers.

As phase four of the Spice Rack Cycle commences in the electricity generation industry, I suspect that global awareness of the need to reduce carbon emissions will combine with a return to the original ethos of localized electricity generation to create small-scale solar, thermal, or wind projects, along with new innovations such as hydrogen-

and water-based generators for the home. Electricity generation could become ubiquitous.

Electricity generation started in the basements of the few with the means to afford it. By the time it completes the Spice Rack Cycle, it will return to the basement, occupy the roof, and spread to a far broader cross-section of the populace.

Finally, let's discuss the humble toilet. In some countries, a significant segment of the population still goes to the toilet in the way people used to before the ceramic toilet ever came into existence. They use fields, verges, and anywhere else they can find. It's not the most hygienic method, but it does have the advantage of turning human waste directly into compost.

The First Industrial Revolution introduced outhouses, where waste was still disposed of locally, but in a less haphazard fashion. This allowed the risk of germs and infection to be contained.

As the Second Industrial Revolution kicked in and allowed for mass production, an entire infrastructure of sewers and sewage plants sprung up to allow for waste disposal on a much larger scale.

More recently, the traditional giants of the toilet industry, such as Armitage Shanks and American Standard, have found their pre-eminence challenged by companies such as Toto, that have started to manufacture electronic toilets.

Toto has introduced innovations such as automatic washers, automatic light sensors, and toilet seats that open and close automatically. These toilets are bringing the benefits of technological advancement to a local level: the bathrooms of their users. Phase four of this process offers the potential to harness digital technology to develop entirely new ways of tackling the challenges of processing biological waste.

A method of transforming waste into pure, safe drinking water has already been tested and shown to be effective, for example. Toilets that are able to assess their user's state of health are probably not far behind. Plus, of course, composting toilets that utilize the best of digital technology to perfect the process of returning waste to the soil, far more skillfully and efficiently than the random use of bushes and hedges will ever permit.

Not every industry is at the same phase of the Spice Rack Cycle, but all industries are traveling that path in some form or another. The greatest opportunity, and the fastest evolution, lies in the fourth phase, and ever more industries are accelerating towards this phase. The capacity to listen will be crucial in determining which companies prosper as the pace of innovation picks up, and which fall by the wayside.

CHAPTER SIX

CULTURE DRIVES TRANSFORMATION

—

*Culture is simply a shared way of
doing something with a passion.*
—BRIAN CHESKY, CO-FOUNDER AND CEO, AIRBNB

For many years, my favorite school subject was history. I found it fascinating to understand how and why things happened. Before long, I realized that the source of conflict, both positive and negative, was often based in culture. I've since made it one of my life's missions to better understand people, cultures, and ways of doing business around the world. The ideas, customs, and behaviors of different groups of people make each place unique, and I believe that studying the similarities and differences can unlock many of the secrets of transformation.

In the modern world, almost every high-profile business leader promotes transformation. Meanwhile, every keen, intelligent employee seeks to remain relevant in a transforming world. Like any change, transformation begins when a company recognizes a need and clearly defines how they will meet that need, and whom they will need to engage to do so. Those are the seeds of culture.

Silicon Valley is one of the most famous hotbeds of transformation on the planet, and its success is driven primarily by culture. This manifests in two forms: Silicon Valley is a geographical phenomenon, a rare collection of extraordinary innovation. It's also a concept that can potentially be exported to other locations and emulated. Many companies wish to encourage a culture of innovation similar to that seen in Silicon Valley, and nearly every progressive city in the world harbors ambitions to establish a similar enclave of technology-driven entrepreneurship in their corner of the world. According to Paul Singh, a successful technology investor, "Silicon Valley is a mindset, not a place."

Silicon Valley, by dint of its previous successes, also attracts enormous quantities of capital. The area is awash with wealth, investors, and funding that make sustaining Silicon Valley's culture relatively self-fulfilling. It also makes attracting human capital, in the form of highly intelligent and motivated people, relatively easy.

Silicon Valley's existing culture is so well established that it has become self-perpetuating. Organizations, cities, and even countries seeking to develop a fresh culture may be starting from scratch, without the name recognition, capital, or appeal of Silicon Valley. Nonetheless, any region aiming to become the next Silicon Valley needs to be aware that capital alone is not sufficient. Culture is a unique and highly important distinguishing factor.

One prevailing element of the culture in Silicon Valley is a high tolerance for risk, and an acceptance of failure as a step on the road to success. Often, individuals who have experienced the failure of a project or startup are valued more, rather than less, highly than those who have never had that experience. It is assumed that people who have tried and failed gained valuable wisdom from their struggles, and have learned from them.

Japanese culture, by way of comparison, is not known for its high tolerance of failure. If a company makes a mistake, as Toyota did some years ago when it committed a number of production errors, executives are expected to bow low and offer deep, humble, sincere apologies.

This is in no way intended as a criticism of Japanese culture, which has many wonderful aspects. Instead, it's an opportunity to survey the differences between a culture that encourages and delights in risk, and one that sees failure as a disgrace to self and family.

The traditionalism of Japanese culture can make it difficult for a young Japanese person to depart from a good career track and join a startup. In traditional Japanese companies, intelligent, hard-working people who follow a solid career path have a relatively assured route to success, albeit perhaps a success that doesn't thrill them in the manner a startup might.

RECREATING SILICON VALLEY—GLOBALLY

There are several places in the world where a culture similar to Silicon Valley shows signs of ripening and maturing.

Berlin operates on a much smaller scale, but the city has an exciting freshness and creativity about it. London is a vibrant leader in the digital economy, although it lacks the sense of a coherent strategy and culture that makes Silicon Valley such a powerful center. Some parts of India, notably Bangalore, are also responding to the call to digitize. The country's massive population and growing mobile phone use makes it an enormous potential market.

Perhaps the most exciting developments, however, are taking place in China. Chinese tech culture has both an impressive access to capital and a far greater acceptance of failure than Japanese culture. I believe it has the potential to rival Silicon Valley in years to come.

The prevailing view of the Chinese contribution to the tech world is summed up by a quote found on many Apple products: "Designed by Apple in California, assembled in China." This quote reflects the perception of China as the world's factory, assembling products designed elsewhere. In some ways, that view is accurate. Apple outsources the manufacture of many of its products to a company named Foxconn, which has operations in China. The components may come from Japan, Korea, Europe, or the United States, but nearly all arrive at Foxconn's Chinese facility for assembly.

This approach conveys the belief that China has the technical know-how to produce cutting-edge electronic gadgets, but perhaps not to conceptualize, design, test, and market them. Dig a little deeper beneath the surface, however, and I'd argue that there's a much more profound cultural transformation underway in China, and that Beijing may well emerge as a true competitor to Silicon Valley during the coming decade, and the same is true of Shenzhen. China has a number of significant advantages. With a domestic market of 1.3 billion people, startups can achieve massive scale very quickly. To put that into perspective, 1.3 billion people is approximately four times the total population of the United States, or twice the total population of Europe.

In the United States, 226 million people carry a smartphone. In China, that number is more than 717 million[17] and is predicted to rise even further. Moreover, the Chinese population is not simply large. It's eager for change and ready to embrace new developments—a movement that comes right from the top.

President Xi Jinping is seeking to move China from a growth model based largely on manufacturing to what he describes as supply-side growth, a model in which China becomes both a manufacturing center and an enormous consumer market. In other words, growing the market for consumer items such as smartphones, and selling those smartphones globally, are both part of government policy.

The combination of a huge potential market, the willingness of that market to adopt new technological trends, and the entrepreneurial spirit of the Chinese people makes the country fertile ground for the growth of tech startups.

Beijing corrals entrepreneurs and engineering talent from two top Chinese universities, Peking and Tsinghua. At the same time, venture capital firms flock to the city to invest. There are several tech hubs in China, but Beijing is undoubtedly the largest. It has the highest level of investment, the greatest commitment from government, and the largest concentration of intellectual capital of any of the new contenders. As a result, companies based in Beijing have the ability to move very fast. All this competition is good for Silicon Valley, too, because it keeps the area on its toes and spurs continued innovation.

XIAOMI AND CHINA'S START-UP CULTURE

Xiaomi, discussed briefly in chapter five, is a powerful illustration of the gathering momentum behind Beijing's startups.

The typical Fortune 500 company takes twenty years to achieve a valuation of $1 billion. Google hit that landmark in eight years. Facebook did it in six. Tesla achieved the feat in five years. Airbnb only took three. Xiaomi, a company most people outside China have never heard of, was valued at more than one billion dollars a mere two years from its inception.

Xiaomi was founded in 2010. By December 2011, the company sold a hundred thousand phones over the course of three hours. In April 2012, that record was beaten when Xiaomi sold a hundred and fifty thousand phones, this time in just fifteen minutes. In September 2012, the company once again topped its previous peak by selling three hundred thousand phones in four minutes.

As a whole, the company sold 7.2 million phones in 2012, sixty-one million in 2014, and more than seventy million in 2015, vying with Apple and Huawei for the largest share of China's colossal mobile phone market.

What really sets Xiaomi apart, however, is the fact that the company's operations extend far beyond the creation and marketing of phone hardware. Mi.com, Xiaomi's e-commerce site, is the third largest of its kind in China. The company also publishes video games, and incubates startups by investing in them and supporting them to create new products, then making those products available via mi.com. They also piloted a financial services arm, which offers people investment opportunities.

The company's business model doesn't necessitate making a lot of money by selling hardware. Often, breaking even is sufficient because Xiaomi's profits come from other products and services, notably credit and apps for the millions of mobile phones supplied by the company.

Xiaomi has a strong track record for creating loyalty, often succeeding in converting customers into fans who willingly contribute to the design of their products. By listening to the ideas and preferences of fans, Xiaomi gleans valuable information and wins their engagement. Fans who have played a part in designing products subsequently evangelize them to their friends, raising demand and enhancing their own sense of being part of the creative process.

This model minimizes business risk, because user feedback assists Xiaomi in making products that people genuinely want to buy. It also allows the company to reduce its inventory, providing the right options without falling into the trap of offering excessive choice.

This, in turn, makes optimizing the supply chain relatively simple, delivering high-quality products at very competitive prices. Every handset that Xiaomi gets into the hands of a user also contributes to the company's long-term bottom line, because customers return again and again to purchase additional services, content, and accessories.

Google hit upon a somewhat similar business model to Xiaomi a few years ago with the introduction of Android. By providing free software, the company makes money by redirecting Android users back to the Google search engine, where they become assets when the company is selling advertising.

Xiaomi, however, has taken the theme a step further, using the incredible pace of development in Shenzhen to constantly improve the quality of handsets, then selling additional services to a vast, highly enthused user base.

Several decades ago, when computer hardware was a novelty, pioneers such as Steve Jobs and Steve Wozniak tinkered in their garages to design and assemble computers. They attended hobbyist events where they could learn from the work of others and improve their own designs.

As personal computers emerged and became cost-effective, business models were based on the ability to consistently produce good quality machines. Brands such as Dell, HP, and Lenovo built their reputations on the quality of their hardware. PCs have always been relatively standardized, and involvement in the hardware market has been an option only for companies that have the ability to operate at scale.

In the era of smartphones, the companies that stand out are the ones that offer outstanding software and service experiences, such as Apple, Samsung, and HTC. In China, Oppo, Vivo, and Huawei are filling this niche. With the advent of cloud computing, almost anyone can develop an app and sell it at the app store, and those that strike a chord with people can be very profitable.

Innovators have always been drawn to the speed and accessibility of software, whereas hardware has remained primarily the domain of a few large companies. Now, hardware has become almost as easy to test and adapt as software. The factories of Shenzhen make producing a new model of mobile phone and testing the responses of people who use it a highly achievable task. The speed at which they operate and their capacity for custom production brings the manufacturing of hardware into the purview of anyone with a little capital and curiosity.

Xiaomi asks people what they want to see in products, incorporates those suggestions, and submits test models for feedback. When a model tests very strongly and the company believes that it will scale effectively, Xiaomi's size and reach becomes another advantage. Extremely high volume allows the company to keep costs down and provide people with hardware they've already expressed approval towards, generating a massive platform of engaged users who already have a relationship with the brand.

It's important to recognize that Xiaomi isn't perfect. In late 2016, the company hit a stumbling block when the company experienced its first significant slowdown. At the time of this book's publication in 2017, it remains to be seen how Xiaomi will handle these challenges. It will be an interesting test of the company's resilience and capacity to continue innovating. Xiaomi has ambitions of expanding into the Indian market, as well as developing the e-commerce and investment arms of the business.

Testing times often open up cracks in previously successful companies, so it will be interesting to observe the strength of Xiaomi's tolerance for failure and capacity to listen effectively as the company confronts its first major challenges since its spectacular growth began to take off.

For their employees, Chinese startups are a highly immersive experience. This is especially true of the "big four" of Baidu, Alibaba, Tencent, and Xiaomi, popularly known as BATX (pronounced "bats").

BATX companies require enormous commitment from employees, symbolized by the working culture known as "996." This means that regular work hours for the majority of employees are between 9:00 a.m. and 9:00 p.m., six days a week.

Most people think of Silicon Valley as a place where employees demonstrate great determination and often work late. In China, that tendency is probably even more extreme. Prior to important product launches, teams are often cloistered in hotels for weeks, where they eat, sleep, work out, and live in close proximity to one another.

Every aspect of their lives is directed towards placing 100 percent of their focus on the task at hand.

A large part of China's progress as a tech hub is built upon the enormous hunger and appetite for success of the Chinese people. Their grit and desire is driving a culture dedicated to leveraging China's enormous advantages towards becoming a world leader in technological development.

The combination of a culture where experimentation and failure are accepted and encouraged, and the infrastructure to make that experimentation available at incredible speed and at a relatively low cost, is equally vital.

China is exceptionally well placed to challenge Silicon Valley in years to come. With the capital available to startups in Beijing or Shenzhen, through both public and private channels, and the Chinese Government's support of the transformation of the Chinese economy, it would be no surprise to see China speaking with an increasingly loud voice in the global tech conversation over the coming years.

MORE THAN CLONING

Few people realize the extent of the cultural transformation that is taking place in China. Many assume that the country remains the workshop of the world, and fail to see how quickly and effectively it is developing a tech industry that learns from the best American tech companies, while simultaneously developing unique flavors of its own.

It's important to realize that Chinese startups and tech companies are not simply taking ideas from elsewhere in the world and cloning them. They are using the success of the organizations they seek to emulate as a starting point, and asking themselves how they can innovate further.

Meituan is another of China's largest e-commerce companies. Founded in 2010, it was valued at $18 billion in January 2016, making it one of China's top unicorn companies and placing it behind Xiaomi as the second most highly valued startup in China. The term *unicorn* relates to companies valued at more than $1 billion, typically tech startups, named for their rarity.

Meituan is China's largest group-buying company. In that sense, it's similar to and inspired by Groupon, and also provides some of the services associated with Yelp. It is also, however, China's leader in online ticket sales and food delivery. It has even grown to be a marketplace of sorts, featuring reviews of products, services, and restaurants. By thinking very carefully about the areas in which they want to focus, the leaders of Meituan have crafted a successful business that uses some of the techniques popularized by Groupon, but goes beyond that template to expand the company's operations into new and profitable areas. In China, this practice is often known as "Internet plus," referring to companies that connect online and offline experiences.

A few years ago, numerous companies wanted to emulate Groupon in China. One of those, in fact, was Groupon itself, which had ambitions to operate in the Chinese market. Instead of trying to outspend its competitors in the sector, Meituan out-competed all the others by adopting a unique approach to customer loyalty.

Groupon provides consumers with discounts that are usually only valid once. The weakness of this approach is that it brings customers into businesses once, using the lure of an exceptionally good deal, but generally doesn't create a lot of loyalty to the companies that sign up for promotion via Groupon. The idea is that people who like a business will be motivated to return, but the reality is that having experienced a business's services at an enormously reduced price, the majority of customers are reluctant to return and pay full price.

Meituan, by utilizing integrated customer engagement

techniques, has found a way to own more of the customer relationship. By offering users the opportunity to write, read, and share reviews, the platform encourages repeat visits. This approach has obvious benefits for Meituan, and potentially for the local businesses that use the company's services. It takes advantage of the group-buying model to attract new customers and create trust, and then leverages that trust into cultivating a deeper, more consistent relationship.

For Meituan, group buying is an entry point, but it's only the gateway towards interesting customers in the company's range of additional online services. It has succeeded in taking an idea inspired by Groupon and building upon it to create a powerful online engagement portal. As a result, the company has more than two hundred million active monthly customers, and hosts twenty million daily users on mobile platforms in over a thousand cities.

Alibaba, by some metrics, is the largest online commerce company on the planet, yet most people in the United States or Europe haven't even heard of it. Taking into account the activities of its sister companies, Taobao and Tmall, Alibaba boasts hundreds of millions of users. Collectively, they purchased 3.092 trillion yuan ($485 billion) worth of goods through Alibaba's online marketplaces in the fiscal year of 2016, principally through Taobao and Tmall. This was an increase of 27 percent from the previous year's figures of 2.444 trillion yuan.[18]

To put these figures into perspective, $485 billion is almost 42 percent more than the $341.7 billion in purchases through *all* US online channels in 2015, and larger than Walmart's total revenue of $482 billion during the same year.

Alibaba's initial public offering in 2014, totaled $25 billion and was the largest IPO ever seen, briefly making them one of the world's most valuable tech companies. The company started with the ambition of connecting manufacturers with customers, and by enabling manufacturers to make their goods available online. Since then, it has expanded enormously.

Alibaba now offers financial services, investments, and the ability to book everything from theater tickets to taxis using the highly popular, Alipay service. The company even invested in Kuaidi Dache, an early ride-hailing app in China. Kuaidi Dache later merged with its main competitor, Didi Dache, to defeat and acquire Uber in China.

Money stored using Alipay can also be redirected towards investment in a money market fund known as Yu-Ebao, which is operated by Alibaba's Ant Financial, and managed more than $145 billion in 2017.[19] Alibaba started as an e-commerce company, but has since expanded so aggressively that taken alone, the company's financial services arm would make it one of the largest financial services providers in China.

It's certainly true that conditions in China are ideal for growth: a population of 1.3 billion people, with a burgeoning middle class, government support for economic growth, increased consumer demand, and a wealth of both intellectual and financial capital. Combine all those factors with an experimental attitude and a tolerance for failure, and China is ideally placed to take enormous strides quickly.

That's not to say, however, that there are no limitations on the growth of Chinese companies. Many are still figuring out how to transfer their success from the Chinese market to the global arena. In fairness, however, something similar could be said of most Silicon Valley companies, which are still trying to expand their success from the United States to the rest of the world.

Nonetheless, China is enormously underestimated as a source of technological innovation, as the examples above demonstrate. Alibaba is a vast, highly successful company, yet it continues to fly under the radar in the

United States. Xiaomi, Meituan, and several other Chinese companies are almost as successful, yet no better known outside China. I've learned a lot from observing them more closely, and I think that anyone who wishes to understand the development of tech culture could benefit from studying successful Chinese tech companies.

Another example of Chinese companies going beyond cloning, and in fact leading a trend that has now reached the United States, is the popularity of conversation as a platform.

Increasingly, many people interact initially with technology through chat programs and messaging applications. The trend began primarily with a Chinese company named Tencent, which is one of the "big four" of BATX, but rarely receives a mention in global business circles.

Tencent also runs a service called WeChat, a mobile messaging service with more than 800 million users, and a mission to improve the quality of human life through Internet services. WeChat extends far beyond simply providing a chat platform, however. It also offers social networking, multi-player online games, web portals, and mobile and telecom services.

WeChat incorporates features of Facebook, PayPal, Apple

Pay, and other popular apps, allowing users to share updates, message their friends, send money, and watch TV and videos, all from a single platform. In China, WeChat has become the default platform for many people wishing to access web services, aggregating services that in most countries are provided by separate apps. Now that WeChat has claimed such a significant section of the market, it's natural for developers to want to use it as a foundation on which to build their own services. These services cover sectors ranging from e-commerce, to entertainment, to information.

WeChat's predecessor was QQ, a reference to the word "cute," launched in 1999. Originally, QQ was created to compete with Windows Live Messenger. It received rave reviews, precisely because teenagers and young people were attracted to the application's cuteness factor. QQ allows people to adopt cartoon avatars while they are online, and in fact, a significant proportion of the app's revenue comes from people who pay to use particular avatars. One of these avatars, a cuddly penguin, also named QQ, is now the company's official mascot, and is hugely popular in China.

By June 2016, QQ was home to an estimated 899 million active accounts, and the platform holds the Guinness World Record for the highest number of simultaneous users on an instant messaging program. On July 3, 2014, 210,212,085 people were recorded online at the same time. Perhaps surprisingly, however, Tencent is looking to phase out the usage of QQ. The product was originally designed for PCs and feature phones, but it isn't considered good enough for modern smartphones. It remains so popular, however, that despite Tencent's plans to cannibalize the app and replace it with WeChat, its millions of users remain loyal.

Tencent and Alibaba illustrate the authentically entrepreneurial elements of Chinese tech culture. They move fast, they're unafraid to experiment, and they are obsessed with creating new products that enhance people's lives. In its early days, Silicon Valley embodied the grit and pure focus on product that is visible in China today. The best startups nurture a hacker culture that comes from the hunger to build something, create change, and make an impact.

Nonetheless, there are some things that Silicon Valley still does better than Beijing, and will continue to excel at for a while to come. One of these is the capacity to grow beyond the domestic market. Just as American startups struggle to enter the Chinese market, so Chinese startups are still largely in the process of understanding how best to transfer their skills and expertise to other cultural milieu. Many have yet to fully explore the potential of international expansion, because they have such an enormous domestic market to explore. By the time they direct their focus towards other countries, they run the risk of discovering that another company has already done what they did to startups in the United States: taken their idea, improved upon it, and developed a solid market share.

Alibaba is an exception in this regard. The company is expending a lot of energy and effort seeking the route to expand outside of China. At present, it seems that their most likely routes will be through supplying cloud computing services to other Chinese companies, helping Chinese people access retail goods made abroad, and distributing Chinese retail goods to people in other countries.

Cloud computing is a major arrow in Alibaba's quiver. Just like Amazon Web Services (AWS) in the United States, the company started by building servers and data centers for its e-commerce retail store and progressed into renting out the additional capacity when it wasn't in use. Many of Alibaba's cloud computing clients are Chinese companies who are themselves expanding into the United States. As they do so, Alibaba is banking on them requiring a support infrastructure for their cloud-based activities.

The start-up culture in China is transforming not only

individual companies, but also the country itself. More and more companies are emerging that challenge the belief that China is a country based upon the production of technological gadgets, but without the expertise to design them or to create innovative business models.

Modern day China is transitioning towards becoming a start-up culture, and doing so with both extraordinary speed and remarkable success.

ALCOA: DRIVING TRANSFORMATION IN THE ALUMINUM INDUSTRY

Alcoa is the world's third largest producer of aluminum. In 1987, the company employed a new CEO, Paul O'Neill. On arrival in his new post, O'Neill asked himself how he could make a positive difference. He soon declared that the company's number one goal was to improve employee safety.

At the time, his approach was considered quite unorthodox. Every time he sat down with an employee, a manager, or a union representative, he asked them what they were doing to improve employee safety. This seemingly innocuous question shifted the behavior of everyone in the company. By the time he retired in the year 2000, the company's entire culture had undergone a radical transformation.

It soon became apparent that improving employee safety required the company to overhaul its entire operations, running them better and more efficiently. People within the company improved the ways in which they shared information, and communicated more transparently. The unions became more amenable to changes. Production lines were run more effectively. O'Neill's determination to improve employee safety led to improvements in almost every aspect of Alcoa's business. It also became a coherent narrative the company could use to guide focus and measure success.

O'Neill's single-minded focus on understanding why injuries happened during the manufacturing process had numerous, unexpected side effects. He put in place a policy whereby workers who had something to say regarding the state of safety at Alcoa were encouraged to contact him personally.

O'Neill told hourly workers that if their managers didn't follow up on their concerns about safety, they should feel free to call him at home, an attitude that eventually spread to all managers within the company. When they realized that they would be listened to and treated with respect, workers began to feel comfortable sharing feedback on how injuries had occurred and how they could be stopped.

As their trust grew, workers also started to offer ideas

about how productivity could be improved without compromising safety, and take responsibility for creating and sharing policies that would reduce the risk of injuries in the plant. This led to workers being given the power to shut down production lines when the pace became overwhelming, both preventing injuries and sending the message that their health and safety were highly valued.

On one occasion, the company hired consultants to assist them in selecting which paint colors to produce. The work was effective, leading to a boom in production of the favored colors, but it also resulted in a shortage of those colors not selected for production.

An employee approached O'Neill with the idea of grouping all the paint production machines together, making it easier to switch from one pigment to another quickly and cheaply. Within a year, Alcoa's profits on aluminum siding had doubled. It was a win on the balance sheet, but more importantly, it was a win for a culture that was originally focused on improving safety, but expanded to create an environment where employees felt safe voicing their ideas and inspirations.

A seemingly narrow focus on safety ended up creating an atmosphere in which innovation thrived. O'Neill was responsible for the installation of what was essentially one of the world's first worldwide corporate e-mail systems, and catalyzed its use by logging in every morning to send messages and make sure that other members of staff were also logged into the system.

O'Neill justified the creation of a new computerized system because it was a way to collate safety data in real-time, and to give managers and employees alike a place where they could share ideas for making the workplace safer. This was the late 1980s, when it was not common for workers to log in to a connected, international network on a regular basis, so the initiative was well ahead of its time in many ways.

Before long, the network was being used to discuss local conditions, sales numbers, and business problems, which people were willing to do because they felt confident that their insights and perspectives would be valued. Executives began producing safety reports each Friday that any member of the company could read, and the open, honest conversations facilitated by the network gave Alcoa a competitive advantage.

O'Neill's determination to make Alcoa the safest steel manufacturer in the world gradually led to an increase in the stock price of more than 200 percent by his retirement. According to Charles Duhigg, writing in *The Power of Habit: Why We Do What We Do in Life and Business*, the benefits of O'Neill's approach persisted even a decade after his retirement. In 2010, 82 percent of Alcoa locations didn't lose a single day of employee productivity due to injury in the entire year, an all-time high.

O'Neill started by creating a culture in which employees felt that they would be listened to and treated with respect. Gradually, that developed into a cultural transformation within Alcoa that permeated all aspects of the company's operations, and had far-reaching benefits that no one, perhaps not even O'Neill, himself, could have foreseen.

THE THREE CS OF TRANSFORMATION

It's possible for organizations of any size to apply the lessons illustrated by Chinese tech culture and by companies such as Alcoa. While every business is different, cultural transformations tend to be driven by common principles. Below, we'll discuss three factors that often play a role in such transformations: clarity, capability, and consistency.

CLARITY

Organizations that wish to transform generally require clear, shared objectives. Alcoa is the shining example of this principle in action. Paul O'Neill knew exactly where he wanted to take the company, and he was able to communicate that simply and effectively to everyone in the organization through a focus on safety. His commitment to the cause inspired others to believe that it was valuable and worthwhile, and enlisted people to his side.

In Beijing, startups are extremely clear about their desire to create the innovations that will move China towards greatness on a global scale and a stronger local economy, and they have the strong and explicit backing of the Chinese Government to do so.

CAPABILITY

In addition to clarity, organizations must have the capabilities to achieve the objectives they set. It's important that efforts at transformation are based on a realistic assessment of what companies can accomplish. Naturally, failing to meet this condition will make it more difficult to create change.

Paul O'Neill's determination to increase worker safety, for example, was based on an understanding of Alcoa's capability of doing that. He invested in training that helped managers and employees within the company to do their jobs safely, and to follow procedures that limited the risk of injury, ensuring that they had both the skills to do their jobs safely and the systems they needed to monitor safety levels. He also invested in infrastructure upgrades, such as painting railings yellow and installing automatic shutdown sensors to stop machines when someone was in danger.

In Beijing, by contrast, it sometimes seems as though there are few limitations. The city is served by the financial capital of investors, and the intellectual capital of China's brightest young people. These factors combine to create a climate in which it appears that tech companies have the capacity to achieve anything they set out to do. Cultural acceptance of experimentation and failure reinforce the belief that start-up companies can learn whatever is necessary to effect transformation.

CONSISTENCY

Leaders wishing to spearhead transformation should consistently reiterate the tenets they seek to instill, both in word and action. This is one of the most important factors in ensuring that a vision takes root in the hearts and minds of those who most need to take ownership of it. This principle applies to organizations both large and small. The larger the team, in fact, the more important it is to keep the message simple.

Paul O'Neill backed up his words with key process changes.

By establishing core initiatives, such as the prototype corporate e-mail system, which he logged on to every morning, and the invitation to employees to call him personally to discuss safety, he made it very clear that he meant what he said. Employees gradually gained confidence in his sincerity and began to behave accordingly, ultimately leading to the production of weekly safety reports from managers and a huge increase in the value of the company under O'Neill's watch.

Beijing's startups and established tech companies, meanwhile, strive consistently to create company cultures that celebrate both victories and failures as opportunities to learn. In short, if you want to transform the culture of your company, you must know what you want to do, make sure that employees have the skills to do what you want them to, and deliver consistently on the promises you've made. It's vital to continue making demonstrable progress towards the realization of the company's vision.

The same applies to a brand's external message. For many years, GEICO, the auto insurance company, has been claiming to "save you 15 percent or more off car insurance." The company continually finds new and creative ways to tell stories based upon this principle, but the essential message is consistent.

Often, business leaders and marketers alike get tired of their messages, slogans, or brand colors, forgetting that they may still be new to many members of their target audience. Consistent messaging, be that around the strategy and mission of a company or the promise of a product and brand, allows messages to truly land and brings organizations closer to desired outcomes.

THE IMPACT OF THE THREE CS

Organizational leaders who create clarity, develop capabilities and consistently reiterate the principles with which they are attempting to transform the cultures of their companies will attract employees who are eager to learn, grow, and transform their own skill sets.

Over a longer period of time, those relationships can blossom into highly productive experiences, with employees becoming both more skilled and more loyal, and the benefit they have to offer the company increasing with every year of their tenure. In addition, as the example of Alcoa shows, transformation in one area of business can readily translate into unexpected and parallel transformations in other areas.

As the Fourth Industrial Revolution progresses apace, companies that develop cultures that support and encourage transformation place themselves in an excellent position both to succeed and to weather any storms that hit unexpectedly. Employees who feel that they are part of a culture they support, and which supports their personal growth, will be both loyal in good times and far more likely to remain loyal when difficulties emerge.

CHAPTER SEVEN

PEOPLE SUSTAIN GROWTH

What if we train them and they leave?
—CFO TO CEO

What if we don't and they stay?
—CEO TO CFO

This chapter is about people. Whether customers or employees, ultimately people are at the heart of everything a company stands for and achieves. Ever since the First Industrial Revolution, people have taken responsibility for powering machines. In recent years, some of those machines have changed shape, and they are increasingly becoming more intelligent. Nonetheless, people will always play an important role in shaping and building relationships with others. The stronger those connections are, especially with customers and employees, the more adaptable a business can be, while continuing to thrive.

Sustainable growth is attainable only with the loyalty of employees and customers. A company that doesn't nurture relationships and generate loyalty may burn brightly for a while, but it will likely go into decline when it alienates the people who make that success possible.

As discussed in chapter one, finding, hiring, and retaining high-quality employees is becoming more and more challenging. In addition, the millennials who now make up 25 percent of the American workforce have a more complex and questioning relationship with their working lives than previous generations.

Exact definitions vary, but those born between the early 1980s and 2000 are generally referred to as members of generation Y (also known as millennials). Baby boomers are part of a demographic boom that started in the United States in 1946 and continued until 1964. Generation X, meanwhile, includes those born between the early 1960s and the early 1980s, while generation Z, also known as generation Zero, starts from the year 2000.

The themes discussed in this chapter apply to people of

all generations, but they are especially relevant to millennials—digital natives who are coming of age in a world of technology with which older generations are less familiar. For that reason, this chapter will discuss the experience of millennials in particular depth.

Millennials are already disrupting the way the world communicates. Their influence will soon spread across all industries, even into more traditional fields. They are often defined by their lack of attachment to institutions and traditions, and they change jobs much more frequently than their parents and grandparents. According to Gallup, more than half of all millennials report that they're currently searching for a job.[20]

As a demographic, millennials are sometimes characterized as disengaged slackers or iconoclasts, but they're also changing the world and the way we see the world. Employers that wish to engage with the best of what the millennial generation has to offer need to recognize the value they bring and understand their priorities.

Just as consumers seek to do business with companies that advocate for causes they identify with, employees are increasingly motivated to work for companies whose activities they believe in. This trend is most pronounced among millennials, who rarely see the companies they work for simply as places they show up in order to take home a paycheck.

Technology has removed boundaries that have historically divided our work and personal lives, bringing a greater urgency to the task of cultivating a working environment in which colleagues are also friends. *Fortune* magazine produces an annual list of the best companies to work for, and the most coveted are almost always those that understand that their employees are as important and valuable as the customers who purchase their products and services.

In addition, the transparency of social media means companies are far more dependent than they used to be on the perceptions their employees, or former employees, share online. Perception is key, and a reputation for treating employees fairly and kindly has a positive influence on the trust of customers and potential customers. By the same token, companies that treat their employees poorly can quickly gain a reputation as an employer to avoid, simultaneously repelling customers they want to attract.

With so many diverse generations to satisfy, each with different values and perspectives, it's never been more complicated to determine exactly what constitutes good treatment. While it's true that millennials, baby boomers, and members of generation X may come to work with very different expectations, however, good management practices span generations.

In many ways, cultivating employee loyalty is similar to cultivating customer loyalty. Companies that seek to meet the needs of their employees and make the workplace a satisfying and fulfilling environment will gradually win the trust of their workforce. This trust can blossom into loyalty with time and consistency.

A MODEL TO ENCOURAGE EMPLOYEES TO STAY

While millennials are not unique, they are often more outspoken about their needs and values than prior generations. For this reason, nurturing their loyalty can be especially challenging. Companies that succeed in creating loyalty among millennials will probably find it relatively easy to satisfy members of other generations as well.

The STAY model highlights the four most crucial factors in determining employee loyalty: **salary**, **training**, **alignment**, and **you**, the manager.

SALARY

It may seem obvious that salary and overall compensation, including factors such as bonuses and health plans, contribute to employee loyalty, but this isn't the whole picture. Just as financial stability is a greater predictor of a company's long-term success than profits built on debts and outside investment, there is no strict correlation between salary and loyalty.

Some of the most highly paid professions, in fact, do not cultivate loyalty at all well. Stock market traders and bankers are judged on their results, richly rewarded when they succeed, but quickly discarded if they fail to deliver. Employees must feel that the salary they receive is fair and reflects their abilities and experience. Companies that fail this test are discounted, but those who pay a little more, especially in a tight labor market, are appreciated. It's not always necessary to pay the most, but it's vital to pay enough.

Another aspect of compensation that makes an impression on potential employees is offering a benefits package that meets their needs. This varies from employee to employee. Some might particularly appreciate health or life insurance, or retirement savings plans; others may be more interested in perks such as flexible working or telecommuting.

Companies that understand this priority make an effort to communicate to employees that they understand and respect the other commitments and priorities in their lives. They provide options, such as free food on Fridays or a dry-cleaning service; that might seem insignificant, but it gives employees the impression that the company cares about them and is making an effort to help them manage their lives more effectively.

Other financial rewards, such as stock options, bonuses, or salary increases also play a part in cultivating loyalty. It's very important, however, to manage these so they improve relationships, rather than diminish them. A small, seemingly ungenerous raise or bonus will promote cynicism instead of gratitude.

Bonuses and raises can be performance-based, but they should always be fair. Upscale grocery chain Whole Foods has been making the salaries of everyone in the company public since the 1980s, because they believe that wage transparency promotes inclusiveness and helps to ensure that fairness is sustained.

Buffer, a social media management company, has taken a similar stand and found the move to be a positive one. The company discovered that people became more comfortable with one another and that openness reduced the sense of competition. In addition, Buffer discovered that their employees enjoyed the experience of being part of a movement towards transparency.

To summarize, salary is important for developing employee loyalty, but that doesn't mean loyalty can be bought. Employees want to feel that their talent and hard work is rewarded fairly, and that the company they work for appreciates them. They like to receive bonuses and benefits, especially those that indicate that the company is listening to their needs and making an effort to meet them. Some may be willing to embrace transparency of salary if they feel that it will contribute to a positive working culture.

TRAINING

Equally important, however, especially to millennials, is the training they receive, and a corresponding access to ongoing learning and development opportunities. To an extent, this is true of all generations, but millennials are especially attuned to the opportunities they have to develop their skill set at work. They tend to be highly purpose driven, and while they may enjoy perks such as ping-pong tables, coffee machines, and free food, those factors won't compensate for a lack of opportunity to grow and develop.

The most effective form of training focuses on employees' strengths and seeks to guide them towards excellence. Weaknesses shouldn't be ignored, but they will probably never be developed into strengths, whereas strengths have the potential to develop infinitely.

There are some generational distinctions here. Baby boomers tend to be more receptive to feedback about their weaknesses and ways in which they can improve upon them. Generally, the working culture during their formative years was more focused on tackling deficiencies. Millennials, on the other hand, seem particularly uninterested in attempting to fix their weaknesses, and want to know instead how their employers can support them in improving the areas they are already good at.

Members of generation X may seek friendly employers who help them to simplify their complex routines and manage personal chores. Millennials, by contrast, yearn for employers that focus on their personal development and well-being. They like supportive managers and disdain faceless bosses, appreciate rewards for good ideas, and prefer flat organizational structures. Fully-funded personal and professional development programs, along with project assignments that make their working lives varied and interesting, also tend to score points with millennials.

It's unclear whether all these distinctions can be accounted for by the differing preferences of different generations, or whether we are simply learning a lot about how best to manage employees in a way that develops loyalty, with millennials at the forefront of the movement. My personal belief is that all of the above management styles will yield positive results, but that there may be generational and personal differences in priorities.

As a young, confident generation with the ability to articulate their needs clearly, millennials present an interesting lens through which to understand the effectiveness of training, but the conclusions we draw from studying how millennials respond should be universally applicable.

Starbucks is an example of a company that takes training seriously, catering to a huge workforce with a significant percentage of millennials. As discussed in chapter four, Starbucks, with 137,000 employees and more than one million alumni of their educational training programs, is one of the largest educators in the United States. In their first year with the company, all employees spend at least fifty hours in a Starbucks' classroom and additional time studying at home and interacting with mentors.

One of the techniques Starbucks teaches is a method of dealing with difficult customers, which they describe using the acronym LATTE. LATTE stands for **listen, acknowledge, take action, thank** the customer, and **explain** how the problem occurred.

Through years of research and training thousands of employees, Starbucks has discovered that teaching them how to be resilient, exercise willpower, and respond effectively in challenging situations has a positive effect both on the mood of the customers and on the experience of the employees. It also increases the sense of alignment employees feel with their roles.

Starbucks has found that by training their employees to handle unpleasant customers, they can give them confidence, defuse potential problems, and simultaneously generate loyalty both in members of staff and in customers who might otherwise have been a source of negative publicity.

For millennials, the experience of personal development tends to be an exceptionally satisfying form of training. It goes beyond training them simply to do a job; it also gives them an opportunity to practice skills that will be applicable in many other situations.

ALIGNMENT WITH COMPANY VALUES AND INDIVIDUAL ROLES

None of this would be sufficient to nurture loyalty, however, if employees didn't feel a sense of alignment both with the values of their employers and with their individual roles.

Decades ago, many baby boomers were content to work for a paycheck. Their sense of purpose and meaning was embedded in their families and communities, and contributing through bringing in a regular wage was sufficient to make their work meaningful.

For millennials, that dynamic is changing. Remuneration is important, but it will no longer compensate for a lack of purpose and meaning in their work. They want to be part of organizations that have a mission. Millennials want to feel mentally and emotionally connected to the goals of the organization they work for, and this shift from paycheck to purpose must be reflected in companies that seek to win their loyalty.

Of course, this movement goes both ways, and employers have every right to determine whether the people they're employing are aligned with the values of the company. This is increasingly a key part of good interviewing. A few decades ago, concentrating primarily on a candidate's qualifications and experience was often sufficient to determine a good fit. That has changed, and an employee who doesn't feel in alignment with the company's broader values can be a toxic presence in the workplace.

"*Why* do you want to work here?" and "What would make you *leave* the company?" are good questions for getting a read on an employee's state of mind. "What do you think the job will entail?" is an effective inquiry for determining how closely your sense of the job's responsibilities and a potential employee's are aligned. It's extremely important to take the time to ensure that employees understand what is expected of them. It's difficult for an employee to feel a sense of alignment with a company when they're uncertain of their responsibilities, or if they are failing to meet an unspoken expectation.

Potential employees, and even current employees, need to feel that their professional and personal goals are aligned with the mission and values of the company. Millennials, especially, feel that the work they do is not just a job; it's a huge part of their life. They are constantly asking themselves whether the organization they're working for appreciates their contribution and strengths, and whether they have an opportunity to do the things they are good at every day.

This is a powerful flip of the popular perception that millennials make difficult, demanding employees. Looked at from this perspective, their attitude makes perfect sense. They want to give themselves fully to their work, and they can only do that with a company where they feel in alignment.

Employees of every generation want to work for a company they trust and that lives up to its promises. It's important to them that their employer behaves responsibly and ethically, treating people fairly and cultivating positive relationships both internally and externally. For most people, that doesn't mean they require perfection. Brands, like humans, are imperfect and are undergoing a constant process of refinement and improvement.

Qualities such as honesty and authenticity are valued more highly than perfectionism. They also allow both employees and customers to make an accurate assessment of whether they are aligned with the brand. In the early stages of their careers, people may not fully understand what they're looking for and where they are most closely aligned. With limited life experience, it can be tricky for them to determine whether a company is a good match.

That's why it's important for employers to monitor this factor and pay attention to how well their employees are aligning with the company, both during the initial job interview and on a regular basis during their tenure. To succeed, employees must feel aligned not only with the company as a whole, but also to their particular role within it. This is often overlooked, and it can be a simple fix for employees who are struggling in a role that doesn't suit their skills or interests.

There are several barriers that prevent employees from feeling a sense of alignment. The first is that they have not received enough training to do their job, which is easily resolved by giving them the training they need.

The second is that their current role doesn't suit them. This is a very common scenario, and it's a strong reason to spend a considerable amount of time on recruiting, hiring, and interviewing.

Employees who are in the wrong role are costly and miserable, so it's very important to do everything possible to ensure that they feel well suited to the demands of their jobs. When I interview people, I ask them questions to discover what they want to do next in their careers, and I use that information to connect them with appropriate vacancies, as and when they arise.

The third barrier, which is usually terminal, is when employees have decided they no longer want to be part of the company, or that they aren't aligned with its values, in any role. In this case, it's usually necessary for them to leave and seek employment elsewhere.

YOUR ENGAGEMENT AS A MANAGER

The fourth and final element of the STAY model is you. Yes, that's right, you. Your engagement as a leader and a manager plays a crucial role in determining whether employees are happy, satisfied, and positive, or whether they're disaffected, bored, and looking for another job.

Your ability to engage with and listen to your employees, to understand their preferences, and to provide them with the salary, benefits, and training they need, makes the difference between the STAY model being an interesting theory, driven by HR principles, and an effective tool, used by all leaders within the company, that brings real benefits.

It's fine to understand that employees need to feel in alignment with the company and with their role, but if you're not asking them how they feel about their current roles, and what ambitions they have for their futures, you won't be aware of those who are struggling or unfulfilled.

As a manager, part of your role is to foster an environment in which honest, open communication can take place. That may involve regular one-on-one meetings where employees have an opportunity to ask questions and share their perspectives. It may mean that you operate an open-door policy and encourage employees to come to you with questions and feedback.

Whatever approach you use, there's no shortcut for investing time in your employees and genuinely caring about their experience. Management is a very deep and personal practice, and it requires a great deal of energy and engagement. You are responsible for giving good performers the opportunity to move to new positions, and for finding ways to improve poor performance. Increasingly, your role as a manager involves supporting employees in career planning, and helping them to think about the steps they need to take towards their next opportunities.

Millennials, for example, don't want bosses. They want coaches. The old command-and-control style of management is outdated and can be counter-productive, but millennials generally respond very well to managers who can help them to understand and build upon their strengths, and add value to their portfolios, both personally and professionally.

This need for engagement also highlights the limitations of

the annual review. Millennials are accustomed to instant communication, using platforms, such as text messaging, Twitter, Skype, or even WeChat. To people who are used to receiving constant feedback, annual reviews seem impossibly distant and abstract. They need regular personal contact if they are to feel that you understand their priorities and concerns.

The companies that we work for are badges of honor. They signify who we are and what we believe in to our family, friends, and the people we meet. They give us a sense of belonging, and working in a culture that mirrors our values reinforces those values and strengthens our sense of engagement.

Managing people is a privilege. It gives you a precious opportunity to raise people up and help them to grow and find fulfillment. At its best, it's a contribution to the greater good. People want to work for companies that contribute broadly in the community and contribute to making them better, both personally and professionally.

Understanding the individual needs of your employees means that you're aware of the life stage they're at, or if something outside of work is disrupting their focus.

If they're fresh out of college, for example, you might keep a close eye on how they're integrating into the company and notice areas in which they particularly excel.

Perhaps they're new parents, in which case you might check on their energy levels and ensure that they have the resources to balance the needs of work and family life. Alternatively, maybe they have a parent or other relative who is sick, and they need to make time to care for them.

These are all scenarios you will only understand if you have a deep, personal connection with your employees, and you are willing to make adjustments to accommodate the different phases of life they are passing through.

We all know managers who try to dodge this aspect of management. They think if they follow the first three principles of the STAY model, they will have no problems with employee retention. After all, they're paying their employees well, training them, and giving them a good job. While this is undoubtedly more than many companies offer, personal engagement cannot be faked, and it can't be overlooked if you want employees to stay. Good management can't be outsourced to HR or others, and it can't be automated.

There are organizations that do a good job of meeting employee needs for salary, training, and alignment, but that only pay lip service to the necessity of listening to their employees and engaging with them personally. Even if they're getting everything else right, managers who are unhelpful when scheduling maternity leave or giving employees time off to care for a sick relative won't maximize their loyalty.

When employees are in alignment both with the company they work for and their personal role within that company, they become what I call morale multipliers. They take the positive energy generated by their experience of their working life, and share that freely with other employees and customers. Morale multipliers help to recruit both new employees and customers and uplift the atmosphere of the workplace.

The flipside of morale multipliers is morale reducers. Employees may become negative because they start to feel disappointed and frustrated with some aspect of their work experience. They may not understand exactly what irks them, but they know they're not happy. They may not be able to highlight or demonstrate their strengths in a way they find fulfilling. They may not be receiving the recognition they need for their contributions. Morale reducers act like a virus in the workplace, bringing down the quality of interactions and communicating their disgruntlement to others.

Every part of the STAY model plays a role in determining employee loyalty. If any aspect remains unaddressed, employees will feel that their experience at work remains incomplete. When the STAY model is practiced assiduously, however, it paves the way for trusting, loyal relationships between companies and employees.

Employees who receive fair financial remuneration and bonuses and the training they need to excel, who feel aligned with the company and their role in it, and who benefit from strong personal relationships with their managers, will be highly likely to remain loyal to their employers.

In the next section of this book, we'll move from discussing employee loyalty to examining customer loyalty. While it's arguably true that the best way to create customer loyalty is to nurture loyal employees who care about the company and wish to see it succeed, there are several ways that companies can use loyalty programs to augment that process.

EIGHT APPROACHES TO CUSTOMER LOYALTY

While developing loyalty goes far deeper than creating loyalty programs, there's no doubt that operating a high-quality loyalty program can be a valuable addition to your business strategy. Every business needs revenue, and the most accessible source of revenue is the repeat business of loyal customers who have an existing relationship with the company.

According to a study by the consulting firm Bain, the cost of acquiring a new customer is five to ten times the cost of retaining an existing customer, and the average spend of an existing customer is 67 percent more than a new one.[21] The same study reveals that, on average, second-time customers refer three people to the business, and customers referred by repeat customers spend 50 percent more than customers who come to a business without a referral.

Overall, the report concludes that improving customer retention by 5 percent can increase profitability by up to 95 percent, so the rewards for a business that does a good job of sustaining and developing relationships with existing customers are enormous.

One of the most common questions clients ask me in my role at Microsoft is how they can provide more value to their customers and improve their relationships with those customers. This is especially true for companies that want to continue to grow their revenue base while the economy is a little slower.

According to Lindsay Kolowich, a writer on marketing trends, loyalty programs are a practical strategy for boosting customer engagement and spend. They're by no means the only way to create customer loyalty. Indeed, for companies that don't take the deeper aspects of loyalty into consideration, they can be little more than cosmetic. Nonetheless, they are useful tools.

A loyalty program is a structured way for brands to provide benefits to customers, so those customers stay engaged with the company. This kind of ongoing engagement can lead to repeat business and to referrals. One study from Gartner, undertaken in 2012 and focused on the insurance industry, indicates that up to 80 percent of a company's ongoing revenue is derived from 20 percent of current customers.[22] Ideally, a company's most engaged customers can become a source of feedback about new product innovations. These kinds of programs take on many shapes, and we will discuss a few popular formats in this section.

According to a survey conducted in 2015 by a company named COLLOQUY, the average American household holds membership in twenty-nine loyalty programs. Only twelve of those, however, are in use, meaning that rewards are earned or redeemed at least once per year.[23] Enrolling customers in loyalty programs that they don't use costs companies time, money, and effort, while the customers lose the potential benefits of being part of the programs.

The question, then, is how companies can convey enough value through their programs to attract a high level of usage. Marketing leaders who have the vision to look beyond simple reward systems and offer real value to customers will reap the benefits. The remainder of this chapter will focus on eight distinct customer loyalty approaches, and outline the benefits of each.

1. ONE POINT AT A TIME

This is a very common loyalty methodology, and one with which you're undoubtedly already familiar. It works by awarding frequent customers points, which translate into some type of reward. Exactly what form the reward takes varies from company to company. It could be a discount, a giveaway, or special treatment such as an upgrade.

Customers may work towards attaining a specific number of points, or they may be able to redeem their point balance at any time. The most effective programs keep the conversion simple and makes access to rewards easy, so customers can always understand what their point total means in terms of rewards. Although this is one of the most common varieties of loyalty programs, it's not suitable for every business. It's most effective for companies that want to encourage frequent purchases of relatively low-value products.

Starbucks uses this type of loyalty program very effectively. Using the My Starbucks rewards program, coffee lovers can enjoy free beverages, free food, custom offers on their favorite items, early access to new products, and easy mobile payment options. Members collect stars by paying with their Starbucks cards at participating retailers, and the stars can be redeemed for rewards at Starbucks stores.

In addition, the Starbucks model continues to evolve, making it more appealing to customers. In certain urban areas, customers can now preorder drinks and have them waiting when they arrive at the store. The company has also simplified the points system. Until recently, customers received one star per order, which led to customers making separate orders instead of ordering together. Starbucks listened and altered their star distribution system to reward total amount of money spent, rather than number of orders.

Loyalty programs such as this one, as well as the technological advances that drive them, have become a significant competitive advantage for Starbucks, to the extent that some of the company's earnings reports in 2016 cite them as a factor in the company's overall strong performance.

To summarize, One Point at a Time is a simple, powerful way of rewarding customers for frequent purchases. It gives them a reason to return to a store or a company again and again, building a relationship while also creating a purchasing habit.

2. ONE LEVEL AT A TIME

The ambition of One Level at a Time is to reward initial commitment and move customers through the tiers of a loyalty program, where they receive more substantial rewards with each tier they crest. This approach is most effective when it strikes a balance between offering obtainable rewards and desirable ones, keeping customers interested as they move up through the tiers.

One thing that makes tiered programs unique is that they tend to encourage customer engagement over a longer time horizon, often many years. This is most relevant for industries or products operating at a high price point, such as airline and hospitality providers.

Delta Airlines, for example, offers customers membership in a loyalty program at a silver, gold, platinum, or diamond level. The more people fly with them, the higher the level of their membership, giving participants access to improved perks and benefits, which demonstrates a deeper commitment to the business. Customers earn a higher status during one year and reap the benefits in the following year, a timescale that sustains loyalty over a longer period.

3. PURCHASE WITH A PURPOSE

This approach to creating loyalty is intended to give customers an opportunity to align their values with the values of the company. The rewards themselves may not even accrue directly to the purchaser, but the model works by giving customers an outlet to express their personal values through their buying decisions.

Eyeglass company Warby Parker operates a program called "Buy a Pair, Give a Pair," which makes regular donations to nonprofit partners that source affordable eyeglasses and give them away to people who otherwise wouldn't be able to afford them. Some of the money is also used to train people in developing countries to give basic eye exams and sell affordable eyeglasses to their peers.

Buy a Pair, Give a Pair was initially started because Warby Parker's founders wanted to give away free eyeglasses to people who needed them, but they broadened their efforts to encapsulate training and employment opportunities for people in developing countries. Simply by making a purchase at Warby Parker, customers are growing awareness and making eye care available in communities where it would otherwise be scarce.

This is not a loyalty program in the traditional sense. There's no membership card, and no benefits accrue directly to the purchaser, but by giving customers an opportunity to align with the values of kindness and generosity, Warby Parker succeeds in generating purchases and loyalty.

Tom's, a popular shoe company, which has recently expanded into eyewear and other goods, provides a similar example. The company's "One for One" system means that every time a product is purchased from Tom's, a person in need is somehow helped. They work with partners around the world, providing tailored products, services, and occasionally logistical support, to communities that are in need.

Purchase with a Purpose is less about rewarding people materially, and more about cultivating a sense of alignment. Customers who contribute to initiatives such as Buy a Pair, Give a Pair and One for One are rewarded with positive emotion and a sense of belonging.

4. PLEASE BUY IN: CHARGE A FEE

Loyalty programs are designed to eliminate barriers to purchase, so what are the benefits of charging a fee for membership?

In some circumstances, a one-off or annual fee actually strengthens a customer's relationship with the brand by giving them privileges and making them feel much more a part of the brand. A 2015 study of 500 leading global brands reported that cart abandonment levels were at 75 percent across the retail, travel, and fashion websites studied.[24]

This abandonment can occur for many reasons. Sometimes, it is a result of sticker shock, an experience that occurs when shipping and other fees raise the total cost of the purchase significantly. Other times, customers compare prices on the Internet, with the intention of doing further research, and possibly making purchases at retail stores. Loyalty programs that charge an upfront fee to bypass sticker shock can reap benefits in the long term, because customers have already made an emotional and financial commitment to further purchases from the company in question.

The system is most applicable to businesses that thrive on frequent, repeat purchases. Amazon is an excellent example. Members of Amazon Prime pay $99 per year to receive free, two-day shipping on millions of products across the site, with no minimum purchase.

Relieved of the inconveniences of shipping charges, and bolstered by the perception that Amazon's prices are usually very competitive, customers buy more. Amazon doesn't release figures, but analysts estimate that the company loses $1 billion to $2 billion of revenue per year from the benefits given to Prime customers. Nonetheless, those customers become so much more lucrative for the company that all that and more flows directly back to Amazon's coffers in increased purchases.

Prime now offers members new benefits, such as access to music libraries, free streaming of movies, or cloud computing space. Increasingly, Amazon is making a variety of products available exclusively to Prime members.

The program works because members feel that the benefits they receive justify the membership fee, and it works for Amazon, because free from the barriers to making purchases, Prime customers spend more money with the company. Some reports estimate that the average Prime customer spends $1,500 annually with Amazon, compared with $625 for non-Prime customers.[25]

REI, Recreational Equipment Incorporated, operates a similar program. Customers pay a $20 lifetime fee to become members of the program. For that, they receive in-store discounts, a 10 percent annual dividend, or 10 percent of the total they spend each year returned to them, and discounts on trips and classes.

Again, the initial impact on the company might seem to be negative, but the cost is offset by the increased frequency of purchases. Asking people to buy in requires that they already trust the brand enough to believe they will continue to shop there, but once they've done so, they are much more likely to favor the company.

They have taken the step of declaring their loyalty and reinforced that sentiment by investing money. They will be highly motivated to maximize the benefits of their commitment.

5. PARTNER WITH NEIGHBORS

Customer loyalty can be developed through the formation of strategic partnerships with neighboring businesses.

These partnerships, sometimes known as coalition programs, can be very effective for everyone involved. They work best when the companies involved can be easily paired in some way, perhaps by location or industry.

For example, a hair salon might partner with producers of shampoo and other hair care products. By helping customers to identify high-quality products or services that are consistent with their own, businesses can communicate that they understand and care about their customers' needs. This is both a convenient method of making purchases for the customer, and a solid upselling strategy for the retailer. Programs like this can also be mutually beneficial, because partners may reciprocate.

Uber utilizes the Partner with Neighbors approach to offer customized services such as food delivery or the pickup of clothing donations for local charities. A lion dance is a traditional part of Chinese New Year. The dance, performed by someone dressed in a lion costume, is believed to scare away evil spirits. When Uber was operating in China, they began offering lion dance deliveries at the appropriate time of year!

Partnering with neighbors can also boost the profile of a business. It can be a way of generating trusted referrals for businesses, because customers who receive recommendations from a company they already patronize are likely to receive them positively.

6. GAMIFICATION

People love to play games. In fact, the playing of games dates back to 3000 BC and continues to be an important part of the fabric of society all over the world. Turning loyalty programs into games, provided the games are fair and fun, can encourage repeat customers. It's important that customers don't feel as though they're being tricked or exploited to win their business.

Nathan for You, a television show in the United States, played on this theme by offering buyers of gasoline the chance of a rebate on their purchase if they were willing to play a game. The game involved going on a nature hike to find the rebate form, but quickly expanded into a two-day journey up and down a mountain, with the aim of discouraging people from ever finding the rebate form. Amusing though it was for the viewer, it was definitely not a successful version of gamification!

Bitcoin is a form of electronic currency that is created and held electronically with no central control or issuing authority. It's also a form of a game, because it encourages people to participate together in their collection. Unlike traditional currencies such as dollars and Euros, Bitcoins are not printed. Instead, they are "mined" by people or businesses using computers to solve mathematical problems.

Bitcoin is the first in a growing category of currencies known as cryptocurrencies, and the founders have turned the gaming aspect of collecting Bitcoin into a means of directly earning that currency.

Many analysts and financial services companies anticipate that the technology underlying Bitcoin, known as the blockchain, will spread widely throughout different industries over the coming years, because it combines the human process of verification with relative anonymity.

7. LUXURY IS SIMPLICITY

This is the loyalty program that isn't a loyalty program. By removing the complexities of a loyalty program altogether, businesses may choose to focus instead on creating a luxurious shopping environment, a pleasurable purchasing experience, or products that are uniquely appealing. Businesses that employ this approach should equally be able to know their loyal customers and reward them, but that process should also be simple, in the same spirit of luxury as the rest of the brand.

Luxury is Simplicity works best for companies that sell high value or luxury goods. If customers are willing to pay a premium for luxury goods, they are more likely to be loyal to the brands from which they've made those purchases. Companies that use this approach focus on building loyalty through the sheer quality of the brand.

The Four Seasons hotel brand has no official loyalty program, so guests may never be consciously aware that their visits are being tracked. Nonetheless, the Four Seasons uses this information to make loyal customers feel even more special on their return.

Plenty of guests at Four Seasons' hotels are ready and willing to rave about their experiences. They do so, however, not for rewards, but because it gives them a sense of having a relationship with a brand they love, and perhaps also to convey the prestige associated with being one who stays at such a high-end hotel.

Luxury is Simplicity works when the brand is highly desirable, and customer loyalty emanates from the desire to be associated with that brand and absorb the experience it provides. Using this strategy successfully also requires brands to make it easy for customers to become loyal fans, and that's an approach brands of all types can embrace. Once again, with a strong brand, everyone wins.

8. INVOLVE ME

This style of customer loyalty program centers on the creation of a community of collectors or fans who feel very much part of the brand. This can generate such strong loyalty that they feel the product or brand exists because they are part of it.

A prime example of involvement is CrossFit, founded by Greg Grassman. Back in 2000, Grassman set out to provide organized fitness workouts that contained a variety of exercise movements, and that wouldn't necessarily require extensive gym equipment.

From its inception, community was a key principle of CrossFit, both online and offline. The company's first affiliated gym was in Seattle and grew to thirteen affiliates in 2005 and 3,400 affiliates by 2012. The company holds competitions such as the CrossFit Games, which have been a part of the calendar since 2007 and have grown rapidly, propelled by a sense of community and the excitement of being a part of something big. CrossFit centers boost participation in the Games, and vice versa.

People who take part in CrossFit get to experience a sense of being part of a community, with everyone striving to achieve similar goals. At first, they may be uncertain whether they're capable of completing a workout, but with the support of their peers, they usually succeed. They leave feeling understood, with a sense of being part of something, and with positive memories that will bring them back.

Involve Me relies upon the highest level of engagement of the customer loyalty approaches detailed here, but it's also extremely powerful, as the phenomenal success of CrossFit demonstrates. People who feel part of something greater have an extraordinary capacity for loyalty.

LOYALTY PROGRAMS THAT WORK

The word "loyalty" is often associated purely with loyalty programs. That's a simplistic approach and, as this book demonstrates, there is so much more to loyalty than offering customers points when they make purchases.

Nonetheless, loyalty programs, when they're in alignment with larger brand values, can be a valuable addition to business strategy. Ultimately, successful loyalty programs are the ones that engage people and help companies build relationships with their customers.

Loyalty programs don't work as the only tool in the toolbox. They're effective only as part of a larger strategy, one that prioritizes listening to customers and providing them with rewards that they genuinely value. If they are implemented as stand-alone programs, they can appear superficial and disconnected from the core values of the brand.

Sustainable growth is achieved only through customer and employee loyalty. People are at the heart of a business's ability to understand the needs of customers, which is why the priorities highlighted in the STAY model are so important.

In the final chapter of this book, we'll examine the ways in which technology is empowering businesses and people to listen more effectively, broadening the horizons of what's possible, and generating whole new avenues of loyalty.

CHAPTER EIGHT

TECHNOLOGY EMPOWERS PEOPLE

Our mission is to empower every person and every organization on the planet to achieve more.
—SATYA NADELLA, CEO, MICROSOFT

How does digital technology empower businesses? One key factor is that it enables the people within those companies to become better listeners.

In a recent PwC survey of CEOs, 86 percent of those questioned said that taking advantage of the advances in digital technology was their number one priority. To put that high number into perspective, 60 percent highlighted demographic trends as a priority, 58 percent named global shifts in economic power, 39 percent cited climate change, and 28 percent mentioned urbanization.[26]

Another study, conducted by MIT Sloan,[27] compared digital leaders with their peers. The study found that, across a range of industries, companies that are leading the way in digital technology adoption outperform those that do not. On average, they garner 9 percent more revenue, a 12 percent higher market value, and 26 percent more profitability.

With the Fourth Industrial Revolution, technology has moved from hearing passively to listening actively. That progression invites a whole raft of novel applications, many of which allow brands to give customers a personalized experience at scale, which would have been impossible a few decades ago.

The most interesting of those applications are the ones that allow businesses not only to compete more effectively, but also to genuinely improve the lives of both employees and customers. Empowerment is such a commonly used term that it's sometimes easy to dismiss it as an industry buzzword. When offered sincerely, however, empowerment is one of the most valuable gifts we can give another person.

Many years ago, as a student in high school, I spent a week volunteering at the Special Olympics. Decades later, I had the privilege of hearing the event's chairman, Timothy Shriver, speak movingly about one of the first races to take place as part of the Special Olympics.

A large group of dignitaries were witnessing a race, and the entire venue fell silent as it drew to a conclusion. A lot of people were tripping and falling, and just as the race reached its final stretch, the front runner fell, clearing a path for the runner in second place to overtake him. In the same instant, however, the best friend of the athlete in second place also lost his footing.

The second-place runner had an opportunity, possibly for the first time in his life, to win a race and receive the applause and adulation of the crowd. Instead of powering through and claiming victory, however, he turned back and helped his friend back to his feet. They crossed the finish line together.

Shriver admits that watching the event, he feared that the visiting dignitaries would react badly to the scene. But, that was true empowerment of the kind that few people are lucky enough to witness firsthand.

While we can't manufacture that level of empathy and

compassion at Microsoft, we make empowerment a priority at all levels of our business. Our entire mission statement is focused on empowering people to use the products we make to achieve more in their lives and their work. This resonates with the way our founder, Bill Gates, has dedicated his life to improving the lives of others through the Bill and Melinda Gates Foundation. His perspective continues to guide our entire approach to creating technology.

Most Microsoft products are essentially platforms or tools, and they only become great when others run software or services on them, or use them as starting points on which to build solutions. The most exciting, at this point, is the rise of cloud computing and the phenomenal range of possibilities it unleashes.

For those less engaged with technology trends, the cloud is essentially a massive confluence of computing power. While some organizations run private clouds to serve their specific needs, most have accounts that give them access to the massive public clouds operated by a few major companies. Microsoft, Amazon, and Google operate the largest and most sophisticated, followed by Alibaba in China.

In the 1970s and '80s, people began building super computers by combining several computers together. Cloud computing operates on a similar principle, but on a much larger scale. By locating many computer services together in a single building or room, cloud engineers generate an astonishing amount of processing power. This power is available remotely through the Internet, meaning that people don't need to set up their own server or infrastructure capacity. Individuals and companies rent space in the cloud, which can be used for anything from downloading and watching movies to running bots and applications.

Security is a common question when discussing the cloud. Some people worry about their data moving from a personal or organizational server to one that resides in a shared location. Yet, these large clouds are partitioned environments with sophisticated methods of keeping each set of data separate. When coupled with the latest security expertise, which larger cloud providers often invest in, along with constant updates and continuous monitoring, space in a public cloud may be more secure than setting up a private cloud.

Nonetheless, for legal and regulatory reasons, some organizations believe they need a cloud within a specific territory. In China, Microsoft has built a public cloud purely for Chinese companies, to prevent data crossing national barriers. A similar approach has been developed in other countries around the world. In the United States, Amazon has built a cloud specifically for government organizations.

In many ways, cloud computing is similar to electricity. It's a utility that's accessible and available almost anywhere. As the technology develops, more and more applications are being built into the cloud, upgrading it and making it more powerful. This could be compared to the way appliances and lighting were created to take advantage of early electricity generation, and to help people see the possibilities.

Perhaps the most exciting aspect of cloud computing is the capacity it offers for businesses to achieve scale rapidly. YouTube was founded in 2005. In the final days and hours before they sold to Google, the founders were literally running out to nearby computer stores to buy more hard drives to plug their servers into, so they could create more space to upload more videos.

At the time, YouTube's growth was limited by the quantity of hard drives the founders could purchase and connect. Nowadays, the kind of server farm that powered YouTube at the time simply isn't necessary. Programmers and entrepreneurs can write an app and plug it directly into global cloud providers, alleviating the need for a costly, bulky infrastructure.

The cloud provides an almost unlimited amount of processing power, meaning that an app connected to the cloud can be accessible almost everywhere on the planet, almost instantly. If it takes off, there's no need to scramble for new hardware. The cloud makes development and growth much more feasible for people who don't have the funds to purchase and run their own racks of hardware.

Cloud computing makes possible the collection and aggregation of a colossal quantity of data, and invites the question of what we can *do* with all that data. Companies are constantly finding new ways to interpret, understand, and act upon the enormous amounts of data now available to them.

Algorithms, which are sets of instructions for computers that tell them how to process information or what actions to take, are enabling data to be processed at an incredible speed. These, in turn, are feeding machine learning as algorithms are adjusted to take into account new information. Over time, computers are becoming more and more capable of analyzing the results of algorithms and making alterations in the outputs they provide.

Cloud computing, by bringing such an immense quantity of data, makes the development of machine learning a reality. It allows the creation of companies, and new ways of doing things, that would have been unthinkable twenty years ago.

ENGAGING CUSTOMERS

The most innovative, forward-thinking companies are harnessing the power of the cloud to enhance the experience of customers and clients, making the process of interacting with websites and apps feel natural and personalized, connecting the global and the local in a way that feels effortless, but requires a great deal of work behind the scenes.

New technologies are making it easier for companies to give customers an experience of being understood and valued. In the Third Industrial Revolution, this might take the form of a file or record containing basic information: useful, but not always personal or comprehensive. As the Fourth Industrial Revolution takes hold, however, it is becoming possible to examine a broad range of data sources, revealing information such as credit history, recent purchases, and interests.

An airline company, for example, might want to learn what credit cards their customers use, and what hotels they like to stay in, so the company can develop better, more personalized experiences that help customers feel valued.

Some data is structured and relates directly to business activities. Some is unstructured, such as an understanding of what people are talking about on social media. This is known as Big Data, and it gives companies a vast amount of information about customers and potential customers. Used empathetically and sensitively, that data can provide customers with an experience of being listened to, connecting them more closely with brands that they purchase from.

Jumeirah owns some of the world's most luxurious hotels and resorts, including the Burj Al Arab Jumeirah in Dubai. While the brand already has a reputation for delivering outstanding hospitality, the company is now taking steps to transform its marketing by using the information it collects from guests to deepen relationships, and they hope to win their hearts.

In some ways, the luxury hotel sector has become commoditized. As the quality of services and experiences at some of the best properties has risen, high-paying guests have come to expect a level of service that is harder to exceed. To counter this dynamic, the Burj is leveraging the data the company collects from its customer loyalty program, and using that data to personalize the way it relates to their customers.

Hotel loyalty programs keep data ranging from food preferences to room choices, and sometimes even the type of computer or phone guests use. Jumeirah hotels use this data to optimize their website. They also use it to deliver tailored and targeted messages to guests with the intention of improving their experiences and maximizing their desire to return to the hotel.

Traditionally, marketing communications have been based upon regional biases, or assumptions about people, due to their age or net worth. These were relatively broad generalizations, which often missed the mark. Jumeirah set out to change that by creating a best-in-class experience in the luxury sector, and it did so by altering the way they communicated with previous and potential guests.

The company thought about the travel objectives of their guests and built what they call a 360-degree view of them, with far greater depth than traditional profiles. That allowed them to anticipate the likely needs and habits of those people, and it provides for them more effectively.

A couple visiting a Jumeirah hotel to celebrate a relative's birthday, for example, might receive an e-mail inviting them to return at the same time the following year and receive a discount when they book the same room, plus a voucher for a celebratory meal. Someone who has previously visited Dubai during retail sales season might receive an offer for a return trip, plus the services of a driver and a personal shopper.

Jumeirah sought to identify patterns of customer behavior and to adapt their service and marketing in light of the new information. As a result of adopting this approach, the company has seen a 50 percent increase in e-mail opening rates and significant year-on-year revenue growth.

In the future, the company aims to be able to identify patterns not only in booking habits, but also in customer behavior *within* the hotel. A guest who often asks for ice, for example, might find that an ice bucket is already provided for them when they arrive.

The overall effect is to create, on a large scale, a sense of being listened to, understood, and served on a personal level. Customers craving the sense of engagement they receive at small boutique hotels can receive that same level of attention, facilitated by data.

OPTIMIZING OPERATIONS

The range of applications available to users of the cloud is extraordinary. Some are using it to monitor production lines and cut down on waste or improve safety. Others are using it to increase productivity.

Oil companies are now capable of reading the condition of wellheads, pipelines, and mechanical systems. That information is fed through operation centers with the capacity to adjust oil flows, optimizing production, and minimizing downtime.

Almost any electrical product, from photocopiers to refrigerators, can now generate data streams and send that data back to the cloud. This presents manufacturers with an opportunity to analyze incoming data and, in some cases, automatically remedy software glitches or dispatch a representative to carry out repairs.

ThyssenKrupp manufactures and runs elevators. The company is using data streams from the cloud to assess the state of elevators and make pre-emptive repairs before failures happen.

Around the world, due to increasing levels of growth and urbanization, the reliability of elevators is an important consideration. Cloud computing gives ThyssenKrupp the ability to prevent accidents, improve service, and reassure customers.

ThyssenKrupp is using this approach to gain a competitive advantage. Hundreds of sensors connect to the cloud, monitoring the condition of elevators. ThyssenKrupp uses artificial intelligence to collect data from the sensors, proactively dispatching repairmen when they are needed. The company's next initiative is to equip field technicians with augmented reality (AR) headsets to guide them as they perform repairs in real time.

In a different industry, Ecolab is a global leader in water, hygiene, and energy technologies. Around the world, businesses in every sector from food service to hospitality to health care use Ecolab products to keep their environments clean and safe. The company employs forty-seven thousand people and has customers at 1.3 million locations in 170 countries. By creating a bank of sensors that monitors every operation, Ecolab is capturing data about every aspect of its operations.

Using an artificial intelligence bot or an agent within the cloud, Ecolab audits the data for irregularities and sends alerts or work orders when repairs are needed. The bot acts like thousands of eyes, allowing Ecolab to spot potential problems before they arise and address them effectively.

This creates a far better experience for customers of Ecolab, who immediately see the benefit of these innovations. This gives customers a positive perspective on the company and the brand, seeing them as innovative and proactive. As it matures, an ongoing monitoring and preventative maintenance service is becoming a discrete asset that Ecolab can sell in addition to the company's core businesses.

7-Eleven, meanwhile, is the world's largest operator and franchiser of convenience stores. The company has a network of fifty-five thousand branches, across sixteen countries. Entering Indonesia in 2009, the leadership recognized both a good business opportunity and some notable challenges.

Indonesia already has a large number of *warungs*, local eateries offering a casual meeting place and inexpensive food. In order to compete with the *warungs*, 7-Eleven needed to offer an attractive alternative experience. To do this, the company employed an analytics tool known as Splunk that enables the collection and analysis of data, which provided numerous insights into the behavior of customers at 7-Eleven stores and allowed the company to better target their marketing.

With the information gleaned from using Splunk, 7-Eleven introduced traditional Indonesian dishes and snacks alongside signature fast foods and drinks. By offering free wireless Internet, outside seating, and techno music, the company succeeded in attracting groups of young people to congregate at their stores, where they inevitably began to spend money.

In order to sustain the competitive advantage acquired through utilizing the data recorded, they have succeeded in developing a smart approach to planning for demand, gathering information from point-of-sale systems and cash registers. They use this data to anticipate product demand, taking into account factors such as weather patterns to determine how many people are likely to visit the store.

As the technology advances, they are becoming capable of integrating more data sources and analyzing that information to make recommendations, or even place orders for items that are likely to be particularly in demand. The potential of this kind of scenario grows further as more technology providers offer AI or machine-learning functionality, enabling retailers to discover even deeper insights from an increasing amount of data.

In one example I witnessed recently, an AI bot simplified the process of preparation for a chef in a hotel restaurant.

From their computer, the chef was able to activate the bot using his voice and assess the demand expected in the restaurant the following day. Discovering that there was a large booking, he used the bot to check where prospective guests were traveling from and assess their local dietary preferences, zeroing in on the types of foods likely to be popular with the group. As a result, the chef received tailored recommendations of the dishes he should prepare.

Following that, the bot accessed the restaurant's previous order history and determined which foods to order, and in what quantities. With agreement from the chef, the bot then placed an order through an integrated ordering system.

Not so long ago, and still today in most restaurants, that process would have required the participation of several people, along with several different systems or tools. The bot was able both to speed up and simplify the process, to the point where one person talking to a PC or mobile phone could accomplish just as much in the same amount of time.

INNOVATING PRODUCTS

As companies become more focused on digital data, and bringing different data sources together, they also have an opportunity to use data to improve their products.

A delivery company, for example, can use data about

anticipated traffic conditions to route delivery vehicles more efficiently, avoiding roads that are busy at certain times of the day, or adapting in real time to avoid traffic jams or accidents. Data from the cloud enables better decision making, which can be transmitted to the driver via simple instructions.

In some financial services companies, machine learning is bringing a new perspective to decisions about which stocks to buy or sell, and when, based primarily on analyzing data from the cloud. Research done by humans is increasingly being assisted by pattern analysis undertaken by immensely powerful, connected computers with access to various streams of data. Cloud-based technologies are capable of analyzing economic data, company information, and even comments made on bulletin boards or social media, and making recommendations accordingly about whether investors should buy or sell a stock.

The field has reached such a high level of sophistication that it has given birth to an activity known as high-frequency trading, in which computers are receiving so much information that they're essentially doing their own trading, based on the data they monitor and parameters agreed on with investors. The margins have become so fine that sometimes investors hold on to stocks for only a few seconds before moving them, an approach that was less feasible without computers.

Afiniti is a company focused on improving the experience customers have when they telephone call centers. They do this by applying artificial intelligence technology to discovering, predicting, and impacting patterns of behavior.

Customers calling telesales centers that use Afiniti's services are linked to the company's algorithms, which pick up what are known as "breadcrumbs" from the caller. These algorithms look for clues to detect the identity of callers and whether they've called before. They assess whether the caller is angry, sad, or happy. They seek to understand the reason for the call.

Using that information, the software prepares the customer service representative, advises them on how to approach the call, and potentially directs it to the appropriate department.

Afiniti can demonstrate the effectiveness of their services, because they alternate between switching them on and off every fifteen minutes. These intervals are used to measure the difference between time periods when Afiniti services are operative, and those in which they are not. Algorithms are updated every twenty-four hours, and are becoming more advanced through learning from the four hundred thousand calls received through Afiniti channels every day.

On average, the company is able to demonstrate revenue gains of 4 to 5 percent through the use of their services, and can profit through sharing the increased revenue with the companies that host them.

According to *Fortune* magazine, Bounce Exchange was the number three medium-sized tech company to work for in the United States in 2016.[28] Bounce Exchange develops a form of software known as enterprise marketing software. Its purpose is to analyze "digital body language" and make websites more convenient and less annoying for visitors, thereby increasing the conversion rate.

The company works a lot with large retailers and publishers, and monitoring factors such as exit intent. By tracking certain cues and signals, Bounce Exchange software can estimate a visitor's intent to leave, and it can dynamically alter the website in response. This is a product, indeed a company, which can only exist in a world of cloud technologies.

EMPOWERING EMPLOYEES

Some companies are also taking the opportunity to

gather data from their employees as a way to improve the employee experience.

Samsung, for instance, is producing a line of next-generation wearables and smart appliances, such as fitness monitors that track key health metrics, refrigerators that trigger a text message when the door is left open, washing machines that assess energy prices to determine the best moment to run a load of laundry, and vacuum cleaners that are robotically-controlled smart watches. Ultimately, the company aims to connect all the devices to one another, providing an integrated platform for distributing content and services.

For employees, Samsung has launched a program named C-Lab, in which those employees have access to data collected from customers using Samsung products, and pitch ideas about how best to use it. The competition is a win-win. Employees get access to data that assists them in doing their jobs more creatively, and they have the opportunity to win a year off from their regular job to research and develop their ideas. Samsung wins through the spread of creative ideas and heightened employee engagement.

The market leader in this area, however, is undoubtedly Google. The tech giant has built a culture based on data collection and claims that "people operations is a science at Google."

Google is constantly testing out ways of optimizing the employee experience, both in terms of happiness and performance, an approach that extends even to the length of lunch lines.

The company set out to determine the optimal length of a lunch line. At what point does a line become so long that it feels like a waste of time, and at what point is it so short that people don't have the opportunity to meet anyone new? Where is the happy medium? Thanks to Google's research, we now know that the ideal length of a lunch line is approximately three to four minutes. The company has also installed long tables to bring people together and invite conversation.

After discovering that women were leaving the company at twice the rate of men, Google initiated a new maternity leave policy. Instead of twelve weeks, the company now offers five months of paid maternity leave with full pay and benefits, and has seen the attrition rate of new mothers drop by 50 percent.

The Google offices are designed to maximize casual connections and opportunities to brainstorm, meaning that the architecture, layout, and even the furniture is informed by data and carefully arranged for this purpose.

In the 1970s, the idea of creating a tech community, where everything people needed was available within a small radius, was new and seemingly revolutionary. Since then, the concept has evolved considerably. At Microsoft, we originally assumed that giving every employee an individual office was the best way to maximize productivity. Until quite recently, it was standard policy for engineers in the United States. Nowadays, that's changing and many of our offices worldwide have been converted to an open plan design, where no one has an assigned office.

Instead, people cluster together with those who are most relevant to the project they're working on. Offices also feature lots of quiet nooks where people can collaborate, meeting areas and café spaces, and often a common courtyard in the center to encourage people to gather. This change was founded on the belief that offices are no longer simply places where people come to work. They are also places where people come to make personal connections with colleagues and partners.

Over the past few years, Google has taken data analysis to a new level in an effort to understand workplace behavior. The company has hired social scientists to study the organization from the outside. The People Innovation Lab is a dedicated area within the firm, where data-based experiments are conducted in an effort to understand how best to manage a large organization.

Every aspect of working life, from how often people should be reminded to contribute to their 401(k)s, to the ideal tone of voice to use when discussing the subject, is studied. The company sought to understand, for example, whether successful middle managers have certain skills in common and whether those skills are teachable.

There was a time when Sergey Brin and Larry Page, the founders of Google, assumed that it was possible to run a company with a completely flat hierarchy, and no middle managers at all. Contrary to that intuition, they've since discovered that good management is essential.

Taking into account scores that managers received in two-sided feedback surveys, and comments received both from employees and managers, they compared the highest- and lowest-performing managers, and found that the best had significantly lower attrition rates from their teams than the least successful. The teams run by excellent managers proved more productive across a broad spectrum of criteria.

Using this information, Google succeeded in identifying the *reasons* that their best managers got the most out of employees, and could teach those qualities to other, less successful managers. They found, for example, that good managers were good coaches and good communicators, that they didn't micromanage, and that they respected and appreciated their team members. With a little training, managers to whom those characteristics came less naturally, were able to adopt them.

Google applies data to every aspect of the company's business, learning, for example, that slowing down the hiring process yields benefits, but that those returns diminish after the fourth interview. The company even examined the best way to reward good performance, comparing the benefits of offering cash bonuses, stock, and time off.

Returning to Microsoft, each employee now has access to their own analytical dashboard, where they can see how much time they spend on different activities, and they can assess which activities have the greatest impact. They can see how much time they spend in meetings, how much time they spend responding to e-mails or connecting with colleagues. While the data is confidential, it gives employees a window into their own performance, and clues as to how they could improve it.

Increasingly, engineers at Microsoft today can see exactly how many times the button or feature they created has been used, allowing them to see which of their products are most popular, and they can receive comments from users and adapt their innovations based on that feedback.

THE BOT REVOLUTION

As discussed earlier in the book, bots are pieces of software designed to automate tasks that would otherwise be time-consuming, such as making a dinner reservation or adding an appointment to a calendar.

Increasingly, these bots take the form of chat bots, embedded in messaging apps or accessed through speaking directly to a phone or computer. They simulate conversation and perform actions based upon the input they receive.

Some bots handle customer service requests. Taco Bell has released a bot that allows customers to order and pay for tacos through an automated chat conversation or using voice commands. Microsoft, Facebook, Amazon, Baidu, Tencent and other tech giants are investing heavily in bots. It may soon become possible to invite bots into Facebook, Skype, or WeChat conversations when planning a trip with friends, and ask them to perform actions such as booking train tickets or checking hotel availability.

Although bots have existed for a number of years, technological advances are now enabling them to become much smarter and more effective. Many are available through cloud services, accessible via human-like names such as Cortana, Siri, or Alexa, and they are essentially an artificial intelligence interface within the cloud.

Here's an example of how interacting with a bot might work. You're taking a trip, so the bot, knowing that you enjoyed staying at the Westin hotel on your previous visit, asks for permission to invite the Westin bot into the conversation. The Westin bot offers you a room, which you accept. With the room booked, paid for, and added to your calendar, your original bot removes the Westin bot from the conversation and moves on, perhaps to other conversations with other bots.

While bots are still a relatively new phenomenon, I expect them to become increasingly popular in years to come. They create a deep, personalized experience through technological listening.

For all the extraordinary technological advances described in this chapter, however, ideally bots and other forms of AI will not replace everything that is done today by people. Nonetheless, they have an important part to play, especially in service-oriented roles. They can assist people in listening more effectively, at greater scale, to solve problems that would otherwise have remained intractable.

Customer service representatives need to be excellent listeners. When they speak to customers, it's important they understand and care about their needs. The tools discussed in this chapter can support better listening and perform mundane tasks that would otherwise distract attention from relating effectively to customers. Technology doesn't replace people. It enables them to be better.

PRIVACY AND SECURITY

In centuries past, levels of privacy were very low in comparison with today. Many people lived in shared quarters or close proximity to one another, where they constantly overheard one another's conversations. Domestic home automation brought a previously unheard-of level of privacy. It became possible for a nuclear family, and more recently a single person, to run an entire home.

Many people are concerned that the rise of new technologies will lead to compromises in security, costing us our hard-fought privacy. It's a concern that technology companies need to address effectively.

As technology becomes more interconnected and gains

the ability to listen and interpret signals, there is a risk that information will be shared between devices and our privacy will be compromised. This is a risk in any relationship, technological or otherwise. The fastest way to damage a relationship is to violate trust. In the twenty-first century, businesses have a responsibility to make sure they are trustworthy in the electronic and digital relationships they form with customers.

That means adopting practices that protect customers' privacy and information. It means storing and managing information safely, whether that's through encryption or other methods.

When a company suffers a data breach, it deals a serious blow to their customer relationships. A prime example is the one that affected Target in 2014. Over Black Friday weekend, the personal information of more than seventy million customers was compromised. The company initially asserted that the number was forty million, and that the information stolen was partial.

Target was later forced to backtrack and admit both that the original estimate of the number of people affected was too low, and that the data stolen included customer names, card numbers, and expiration dates, along with address details, phone numbers, and e-mail addresses.

The loss of the data was bad enough, but Target's slow admission of the facts compounded the situation. The company tried to offer affected customers a year of free credit monitoring and identity theft protection, but the damage had been done. Target's stock price dropped, sales declined, and the impact on customer relationships was catastrophic. The company failed to take enough proactive steps to protect their customers' information, and this resulted in a perceived violation of trust.

For companies that seek to listen effectively, serve customers well, and build trusting relationships, digital technology can be a tool that empowers them to do so at greater scale. Used intelligently, new technologies can open new horizons and facilitate deeper connections with customers, smarter operations, improved products, and more engaged employees. Used improperly, however, the ability to collect data, and in effect listen digitally, can fuel mistrust and dissatisfaction on a large scale.

Companies that wish to thrive in the twenty-first century need to tap into the enormous potential of digital technology, yet they must also remain aware that with great power comes great responsibility.

CONCLUSION: THE LOYAL ORGANIZATION

Satisfied employees mean satisfied customers, which leads to profitability.
—ANNE M. MULCAHY, CEO, XEROX

The next time you sit down to discuss growth in your company, and your colleagues are focused on how to attract new customers or new employees, consider instead shifting the discussion to the people who are already part of the organization. A company with loyal employees often attracts satisfied customers, and together those factors create the strongest growth magnet.

Successful companies listen to their customers and employees. Those that listen well can build trust and create loyalty. In a world where customers and employees have more choice than ever, loyalty could not be more important.

"I used to think I should treat people the way I wanted to be treated," says Tim Ryan, the new US Chairman of PwC. "But really, I need to treat people the way they want to be treated." That's a subtle shift, he confirms, one that requires a willingness to listen. "It's good, I'm growing."

We're now entering an era in which technology can facilitate deep listening. Deep listening is a method of collecting increasing amounts of data and finding connections between them: improving customer engagement, optimizing operations, improving products, and developing lasting loyalty in employees.

Since the dawn of industrialization, technology has provided tools to make businesses better. As we enter the Fourth Industrial Revolution, we stand at the dawn of an age of digital creation and ubiquitous consumption, enabled by cloud computing and machine learning.

While the digital era provides many things, it's primarily characterized by new ways of doing business using technology and the mass proliferation of data that can be collected and monitored. Sensors and connections are capturing more and more inputs, and our capacity to listen via technology is greater than it ever has been. Just two years ago, there were perhaps a hundred companies with an interest in machine learning. Now, in 2017, there are thousands. Every industry, from food to automobiles, from computing to energy discovery and production, is being touched by this transformation. Every company is becoming a digital company.

The good news is that digital transformation is fiercely egalitarian. The concept of emerging markets is already becoming obsolete. Countries in the BRICS block (Brazil, Russia, India, China, and South Africa), thought until recently to be the primary emerging economies, are nearly all facing economic challenges, stagnation, or political instability.

They still present enormous economic opportunities, but our definition of an emerging economy has changed. In China, specifically, the market is evolving. The country is moving from an economy based solely upon production to one based also upon innovation and consumption. Technology is becoming an equalizing force, which has the potential to create fresh opportunities for businesses—and nations—of all sizes. Technological listening is advancing and successful organizations are embracing the possibilities it offers.

This book highlights examples of companies that are successfully using new technologies, and hopefully also raises awareness of the new ways in which some of these new technologies can be used. The digital era is one in which the experience of being listened to and understood, which was once thought to be the preserve of the local general store, can be scaled across much larger organizations and locations, serving many more customers.

Digital tools are empowering employees to create experiences that make customers feel listened to in an intimate way. Organizations that succeed in this new era will be the ones that have not only the tools to listen effectively, but also a culture of listening throughout the organization. Technology invites companies to reconsider the ways they do business. Firms that fail to take advantage of these opportunities, however, risk being outcompeted and losing market share.

Pick up a business magazine and you'll soon realize how universal the conversation about digital transformation is becoming. The power of new technologies built on Big Data and cloud computing are key areas of discussion, and companies that fail to take advantage of what they offer will likely be obscured by competitors.

Companies that grasp the possibilities of digital tools, however, place themselves in a prime position to attract top talent in a highly competitive marketplace. A workforce that is constantly learning and improving in pursuit of a specific purpose is the most valuable resource available to an employer. Without loyal employees, it will be very difficult to attract, retain, and grow a loyal customer base that stays connected with the company as it transforms.

Over the next decade, we'll see more and more industries transform themselves to take advantage of the digital era. New companies will be created, others will grow and develop, and still others will fade away.

None of this is to suggest that human relationships will be superseded by technology. In a world where technology is listening deeply, it will ideally supplement and support human relationships, not replace them.

Listening has always been a critical tool for generating respect and understanding. Faced with a wave of digital transformation, we now have access to exciting tools that allow us to listen better than ever.

In a world of choice, technology will help people make choices that align with their values, guiding them to companies that they feel most accurately represent their principles, and to brands with which they feel connected. When we combine the traditional values that nurture loyalty with the huge potential of digital technology, we empower ourselves to build stronger relationships and more fruitful connections.

In many ways, the currency of the twenty-first century *is* people, and what they can create through their skills and loyalty when they are empowered to do so.

I hope this book has broadened your perspective on both the importance of listening and the role that technology can play in helping us all to listen more expertly. I hope it has provided you with a context for understanding the massive transformation that digital technology is already creating in the way we listen, and a framework for interpreting business news and commentary.

Above all, I hope this book has inspired you to listen more deeply to your customers and your employees, to exercise your curiosity, and to think about how you can lead the way in transforming your own company or industry. Ultimately, a commitment to better listening and developing loyalty can lead us towards building a better world.

ACKNOWLEDGMENTS

Writing a book is never an easy project, especially when combined with a full-time job. With only limited nights and weekends to write and living in a foreign country, I always felt self-applied pressure to be out experiencing local culture and exploring new neighborhoods, not sitting inside researching or writing.

Yet, I believe strongly in gratitude and am all the more grateful for so many who helped me to have the experiences and capture the learning contained in this book.

My CEO at Microsoft, Satya Nadella, always advocates that employees should use the company as their own personal platform. Under his leadership, I'm grateful to have had this incredible platform. Equally, I'm grateful to those with whom I've had a chance to work and learn from.

Jeff Raikes and Chris Capossela made a bet in hiring me originally into the company, and Jean-Philippe Courtois helped expose me to our global operations and the customers, partners, and employees that came along with it. Ralph Haupter invited me to join his organization in Asia and empowered me to build a new business area in China.

These leaders are only a few of so many who have helped encourage my growth and allowed me to have an impact over the years. My team members, employees, and colleagues have helped me to practice and learn from many of the management concepts shared here. Our hundreds of college and MBA hires who I mentor, have also helped me learn the millennial mindset through their questions and feedback.

A countless number of CEOs, CFOs, CIOs, and others around the world who are my "customers," have become more like partners and friends over the years. It is in listening to them that I have learned so much, which helped me to develop the content shared here. Out of respect for their privacy and some of the confidential business strategies they've shared, I won't list their names. They know who they are.

Beth Brooke-Marciniak gave me opportunity and professional encouragement at an early stage of my career, when I needed it most. Steve Orlins helped me to see the enormous potential in China and encouraged me to make the move to see for myself.

Friends and family are truly my greatest asset, and they have helped me become the person I am today. Many of them, especially Sheila Gulati and John Pinette, offered remarkably sage advice as reviewers. I feel fortunate to have such talented professionals in my personal life.

My editor, Robert Wolf Petersen, has been invaluable in this process, helping me to synthesize and make sense of what started out as a much longer text and turn it into something clear and structured.

A very sincere thank you to all those in my life who offer support, constructive criticism and friendship. I try to be a leader who listens, and it is from listening to you that I become a better person.

ABOUT THE AUTHOR

AARON PAINTER is a global executive who is passionate about how listening empowers people and organizational growth. Having lived and worked in six countries across four continents, Painter exemplifies a new generation of global leaders. He has codified the frameworks and cultural attributes of effective leadership, and by using these practices, he has built businesses across the world—delivering positive outcomes in multiple turnarounds, hyper-growth startup products, and large-scale enterprise sales and marketing.

Painter is vice president and general manager at Microsoft in Beijing, China. He leads a broad organization of sales, marketing, product development, and partner management professionals who engage customers to develop technology-based business solutions. His team provides cloud-based ERP and CRM software solutions to transform how modern enterprises run their operations, and how they deliver data-based decision making to better connect with their customers. These integrated solutions are delivered based on the Microsoft Dynamics 365 product line, together with strategic alliance partners such as Adobe, LinkedIn, and other industry-specific solution integrators and business consultants.

Previously, Painter led Microsoft's corporate accounts and partner groups in Hong Kong. Within a year, he spearheaded the turnaround of this organization, and his team transformed the business unit to be recognized as the top-performing division in Asia. Based in France, Painter also served as chief of staff to the president of Microsoft International. In this role, he drove key business-development initiatives and both designed and implemented emerging market-growth strategies, while managing daily operations and communications for Microsoft's global sales, marketing, and services division in more than 190 countries. When stationed in Brazil, Painter served as general manager of the Windows Business Group, where he doubled the commercial business over a two-year period. Under his leadership, Brazil grew from the sixth to the third largest PC market in the world, as his team improved all aspects of business performance, product marketing, local product development, and operations. Painter began his Microsoft career in Redmond, Washington, as a product manager for the Office business. Prior to joining Microsoft, he spent time in several consulting and public-sector organizations.

Painter has built a reputation for his ability to combine international practices with local insights. He builds world-class teams that innovate and execute creatively—with humility, integrity, and enthusiasm. Painter is also an executive sponsor for Microsoft's rising millennial workforce of recent hires from top undergraduate and MBA programs. He is a sought-after speaker, advisor, and consultant to CEOs and business leaders who are seeking to achieve sustained business growth in the digital era. On a personal level, Painter prides himself on being a curious and sincerely interested global citizen—having traveled to more than one hundred countries, he continues to seek out new people, cultures, and ways of doing business.

For more information, please visit: www.aaronpainter.com.

REFERENCES

1. http://www.economist.com/news/special-report/21648171-far-declining-family-firms-will-remain-important-feature-global-capitalism
2. https://www.emc.com/leadership/digital-universe/2014iview/executive-summary.htm
3. https://hackernoon.com/ceos-survey-on-digital-transformation-in-2017-by-gartner-c2d6e842f86c
4. https://www.gartner.com/doc/3275917/-ceo-survey-year-digital
5. http://www.gallup.com/reports/199961/state-american-workplace-report-2017.aspx?utm_source=SOAW&utm_campaign=StateofAmericanWorkplace&utm_medium=2013SOAWreport
6. http://www.nielsen.com/us/en/insights/news/2012/consumer-trust-in-online-social-and-mobile-advertising-grows.html
7. https://www.youtube.com/watch?v=fW8amMCVAJQ
8. http://archive.fortune.com/magazines/fortune/fortune500_archive/full/1955/
9. http://www.aei.org/publication/fortune-500-firms-in-1955-vs-2014-89-are-gone-and-were-all-better-off-because-of-that-dynamic-creative-destruction/

10. https://www.bloomberg.com/view/articles/2016-04-29/amazon-and-facebook-are-big-spenders-on-r-d
11. http://www.strategyand.pwc.com/innovation1000
12. http://www.bbc.com/news/business-16611040
13. https://hbr.org/2007/05/why-employees-are-afraid-to-speak
14. https://www.americanprogress.org/issues/economy/reports/2012/11/16/44464/there-are-significant-business-costs-to-replacing-employees/
15. https://www.fastcompany.com/1802731/four-year-career
16. http://www.inc.com/justin-bariso/elon-musk-takes-customer-complaint-on-twitter-from-idea-to-execution-in-6-days.html
17. https://en.wikipedia.org/wiki/List_of_countries_by_smartphone_penetration
18. http://www.alibabagroup.com/en/news/press_pdf/p160505.pdf
19. https://www.chinamoneynetwork.com/2017/04/27/alibabas-yuebao-becomes-first-chinese-fund-management-firm-with-over-rmb1-trillion-in-assets
20. http://www.gallup.com/businessjournal/191459/millennials-job-hopping-generation.aspx
21. http://www.bain.com/Images/Value_online_customer_loyalty_you_capture.pdf
22. http://www.gartner.com/newsroom/id/1971816
23. https://www.colloquy.com/latest-news/2015-colloquy-loyalty-census/
24. https://blog.salecycle.com/stats/remarketing-report-q1-2015/
25. https://files.ctctcdn.com/150f9af2201/bf283d9e-4cbb-4306-8645-b2dc9a16d805.pdf
26. http://www.pwc.com/us/en/ceo-survey-us/digital-transformation.html
27. https://www.capgemini.com/resource-file-access/resource/pdf/The_Digital_Advantage__How_Digital_Leaders_Outperform_their_Peers_in_Every_Industry.pdf
28. http://fortune.com/best-medium-workplaces-in-technology/bounce-exchange-3/

Printed in Great Britain
by Amazon